KB249405

The Adventures of MAYA the BEE

The Adventures of Maya the Bee

초판 제 1쇄 인쇄 | 2010년 7월 5일
초판 제 1쇄 발행 | 2010년 7월 10일
지은이 | Waldemar Bonsels
발행인 | 정형화
마케팅 | 문승찬
디자인 | 이오커뮤니케이션
표지 일러스트 | 박은경
발행처 | (주)올바른 창조
주소 | 서울시 서초구 양재동 10-41
율촌빌딩 4층
전화 | 02-568-7070 팩스 | 02-568-7176
인터넷 홈페이지 www.drjungeclass.com
이메일 scm8820@naver.com

ISBN 978-89-964289-0-9 (세트)
978-89-94529-01-1 04740

The Adventures of MAYA the BEE

By Waldemar Bonsels

닥터정 E 클래스

Preface

닥터 정의 English Classic 100 선

캐나다에서 아이 둘의 영어공부를 영어독서를 통해 한 경험과 그 때 만든 자료를 통해 2005년 서울 강남구 대치동에 '닥터정이클래스'라는 영어도서관을 만들었습니다. 아무튼 영어독서를 통해 영어를 공부하는 곳이 흔하지 않아서 그럭저럭 경영은 되었고 또 한 두 군데씩 지점도 생기게 되었습니다.

그러나 항상 제 마음속에 아쉬운 점이 남아 있었습니다. 영어도서관이든 학원이든 그 곳에 와서 영어공부를 하려면 돈이 들지 않을 수 없는 것이죠. 적은 돈으로 영어를 제대로 공부하고 그리고 또한 생각의 깊이를 키울 수 있는 방법은 없을까! 많은 고민을 했습니다. 그 해답은 결국 좋은 책을 조금 쉽게 집에서 읽을 수 있게 하는 것입니다.

그럼 좋은 책은 무엇일까요? 고전이죠. 고전에는 삶의 지혜와 즐거움이 담겨져 있으니까요. 그래서 고전을 통하여 영어를 제대로 배우고 고전을 통하여 삶의 지혜와 즐거움을 얻기를 바라는 간절한 마음에서 닥터정의 **English Classics 100선**을 준비하게 되었습니다.

100선을 하나 하나 준비하는 과정 중 저 자신도 즐거움과 지혜를 배우게 되었음을 여러분께 인정하지 않을 수 없습니다. 단지 영어 공부가 아니라 삶을 지탱하는 정신의 힘과 깊이를 이 고전을 통하여 체험할 수 있기를 진정으로 바랍니다.

제가 이 책을 보기를 원하는 연령대는 초등학생부터 대학생까지입니다. 만약 영어교육에 종사하시는 분이 계신다면 그 분들은 반드시 읽어보기를 권합니다. 그리고 영어공부에 관심이 있는 성인도 읽어보기를 바랍니다. 특히 외국유학(영어권)을 가는 학생들은 반드시 읽고 가기를 바랍니다. 이 고전 중에는 사실 제가 축약본으로 보거나 대강 내용만 알고 읽어보지 못한 것도 적지 않았습니다. 그러한 고전을 제가 다시 읽고 준비하는 과정을 거치면서 왜 이러한 책을 특히 대학(학과)을 선택하기 전인 10대 후반까지 읽지 못했는가, 아니면 조금 늦더라도 20대 초반까지 읽지 않았는가 하는 후회 아닌 후회를 하게 되더군요.

제가 느끼고 체험하는 고전의 즐거움을 독자 여러분들도 같이 느끼고 그 체험과 느낌을 통하여 독자 여러분의 삶도 더 풍성하고 즐겁게 되기를 간절히 바라고 바랍니다.

닥터정 정형화

특징과 공부 방법

왜 '닥터 정의 English Classics 100선' 을 사야 할까요?

왜 수많은 출판사에서 번역판이나 축약판, 아니면 원서를 출간함에도 닥터 정의 English Classics 100선을 제가 다시 출간하게 되었을까요?

그것은 직독직해 만이 가장 완전한 영어 공부 형태이기 때문입니다. 영어의 중요한 어휘를 문장을 통해 유추하는 것이 가장 효율적이고 가장 정확히 어휘의 뜻을 이해할 수 있기 때문입니다. 영어의 원문이 우리 나라말로 어떻게 표현되는지, 어떤 상황에서 영어를 사용하는지, 직독직해 형식만이 그것을 정확히 이해할 수 있게 하기 때문입니다.

예 **External** heat and cold had little influence on Scrooge. No warmth could warm, no wintry weather **chill** him. No wind that blew was bitterer than he, no falling snow was more intent upon its purpose, no **pelt**ing rain less open to **entreaty**

External: 외부의 / influence on: 영향(on) / warmth: 온기, 따뜻함 / wintry: 겨울의 / chill: 춥게 하다, 한기 / bitterer: 매서운, 쓴 / no falling snow was more intent: (내리는 어떤 눈도 (스크루지의) 집념 보다 강할 수 없다) / intent: 집중된 / purpose: 목적 / pelt: 내던지다, 비가 억수같이 내리다 / open: 공공연한 / entreaty: 탄원, 애원

예에서 보듯이 영어 본문을 읽어가면서 모르는 단어나 이해 안가는 부분을 바로 한글로 이해하면서 영어를 읽어갈 때 영어와 한글이 서로 다른 것이 아니라 같은 하나의 언어구나 라고 느끼게 될 것이고 바로 그렇게 함으로 동시통역(영어의 완성)에 도달하게 되기 때문입니다. 본문 중에서 볼드체로 표시된 내용은 시험(SAT나 Toefl)에 나오는 중요 단어들입니다.

또한 축약이 아니라 완역한 내용만이 책에 대한 더 깊은 이해와 책 내용에 대한 더 깊은 사고를 가능하게 하기 때문에 축약판이 아니라 원전을 실었습니다. 영어도 중요하지만 그 못지 않게 사고력도 중요하기 때문이고 원전을 이해하는 것이 결국 축약판을 읽고 이해하는 것 보다 공부(영어+국어)에 더 도움이 되기 때문입니다.

이 책은 다음과 같은 방법으로 읽어 보시기 바랍니다.

1. 책을 정성 들여 읽는다. (되도록 해석을 보지 않고)
2. 읽은 책을 오디오와 함께 듣고 읽는다.
3. 오디오만 들어 본다.
4. 마지막 필수 어휘 부분은 반드시 다 알 때까지 읽고 또 읽는다.

즉 책을 3번 읽을 각오로 공부하시기 바랍니다.

꿀벌 마야는 모험심과 호기심이 대단한 꿀벌입니다. 그래서 자기의 고향을 떠나 저 넓은 세상을 탐험하게 되죠. 용감하고 자부심 강한 마야의 모습을 여러분은 이 책에서 경험할 수 있을 것입니다.

세상은 호기심과 모험심이 있고 도전의식이 있는 사람에게는 무한한 보물창고입니다. 죽음에 대한 두려움도 끝에 대한 불안함도 그런 사람에게는 다가가지 못합니다. 여러분 모두모두가 이 꿀벌 마야처럼 용기 있고 자존심을 갖고 자기 가족이나 민족을 사랑하고 살기를 바랍니다.

이 책을 지은 저자는 독일 사람인 발데마르 본젤스(Waldemar Bonsels, 1880~1952) 입니다. 저자는 아름다운 독일의 한 농촌 마을에서 반 평생을 살았습니다. 젊을 때는 인도, 아프리카, 아시아 등도 여행했죠. 그런 여행 경험이 이 책을 쓰는 기반이 되었을 것입니다.

저는 여러분이 이 아름다운 세상에서 용기와 열정을 가지고 마음껏 여러분의 뜻을 펼쳐가며 살기를 바랍니다. 그러기 위해 열심히 영어 책 많이 읽고 들읍시다.

Contents

CHAPTER 01

FIRST FLIGHT

The elderly (나이가 많은) lady-bee who helped the baby-bee Maya when she awoke (깨어났다) to life and slipped (살짝 나가다, 미끄러지다) from her cell (작은 방, 벌집, 세포) was called Cassandra and commanded (존경이나 관심 등을 끌다, 명령하다) great respect (존경) in the hive (벌집). Those were exciting days. A **rebellion** (반란) had broken out (발생했다) in the nation (국가) of bees, which the queen was unable (~할 수 없는) to suppress (진압하다).

While the experienced (경험 많은) Cassandra wiped (닦다) Maya's large bright eyes and tried as best she could to arrange (정돈하다) her delicate (부드러운) wings, the big hive (벌떼) hummed (벌이 윙윙거리다) and buzzed (윙윙 소리를 내다) like a threatening (위협적인) thunderstorm (심한 뇌우), and the baby-bee found it very warm and said so to her companion (동행자).

Cassandra looked about troubled (불안한 듯), without replying (대답하다).

It astonished her that the child so soon found something to **criticize**. But really the child was right: the heat and the pushing and crowding were almost **unbearable**. Maya saw an endless **succession** of bees go by in such **swarm**ing haste that sometimes one climbed up and over another, or several rolled past together **clot**ted in a ball.

Once the queen-bee approached. Cassandra and Maya were **jostle**d aside. A drone, a friendly young fellow of **immaculate** appearance, came to their **assistance**. He nodded to Maya and stroked the shining hairs on his breast rather nervously with his foreleg. (The bees use their forelegs as arms and hands.)

"The crash will come," he said to Cassandra. "The revolutionists will leave the city. A new queen has already been **proclaim**ed."

Cassandra scarcely noticed him. She did not even thank him for his help, and Maya felt keenly **conscious** that the old lady was not a bit nice to the young gentleman. The child was a little afraid to ask questions, the impressions were coming so thick and fast; they threatened to **overwhelm** her. The general excitement got into her blood, and she set up a fine, distinct buzzing.

"What do you mean by that?" said Cassandra. "Isn't there noise enough as it is?"

Maya **subside**d at once, and looked at Cassandra questioningly.

"Come here, child, we'll see if we cannot quiet down a bit." Cassandra took Maya by her gleaming wings, which were still soft and new and marvelously **transparent**, and shoved her into an almost **deserted** corner beside a few honeycombs filled with honey.

Maya stood still and held on to one of the cells.

"It smells delicious here," she observed.

Her remark seemed to **fluster** the old lady again.

"You must learn to wait, child," she replied. "I have brought up several hundred young bees this spring and given them lessons for their first flight, but I haven't come across another one that was as **pert** and forward as you are. You seem to be an exceptional nature."

Maya **blush**ed and stuck the two dainty fingers of her hand in her mouth.

"Exceptional nature—what is an exceptional nature?" she asked shyly.

"Oh, that's not nice," cried Cassandra, referring not to Maya's question, which she had scarcely heeded, but to the child's sticking (찌름) her fingers in her mouth. "Now, listen. Listen very carefully to what I am going to tell you. I can **devote** (바치다, 전념하다) only a short time to you. Other baby-bees have already slipped out, and the only helper I have on this floor is Turka, and Turka is dreadfully (끔찍하게) overworked (지나치게 일 시키다) and for the last few days has been **complain**ing (불평하다) of a buzzing (귀가 윙윙거림) in her ears. Sit down here."

Maya obeyed (복종하다), with great brown eyes fastened (시선을 집중하다, 고정하다) on her teacher.

"The first rule (규칙) that a young bee must learn," said Cassandra, and sighed, "is that every bee, in whatever it thinks and does, must be like the other bees and must always have the good (좋음, 선) of all in mind. In our order (체제, 도리, 이치) of society (사회), which we have held to be the right one from time **immemorial** (먼 옛날의) and which couldn't have been better preserved (보존하다) than it has been, this rule is the one fundamental (근원의) basis (기본) for the well-being (행복, 안녕) of the state (국가). To-morrow you will fly out of the hive, an older bee will accompany (같이 가다) you. At first you will be allowed (허락 받다) to fly only short stretches (범위, 한도, 거리) and you will have to observe (관찰하다) everything, very carefully, so that (그래서) you can find your way back home again. Your companion (동료) will show you the hundred flowers and blossoms (과일의 꽃) that yield (낳다, 가져오다) the best nectar ((꽃의) 꿀). You'll have to learn (배우다)

them by heart(외우다). This is something no bee can escape(벗어나다) doing.—Here, you may as well(~하는 게 낫다) learn the first line(줄, 글의 행) right away—clover and honeysuckle(인동초). Repeat it. Say 'clover and honeysuckle.'"

"I can't," said little Maya. "It's awfully hard. I'll see the flowers later anyway."

Cassandra opened her old eyes wide and shook(흔들었다) her head.

"You'll come to a bad end," she sighed. "I can foresee(미리 알다) that already."

"Am I supposed later on to gather(모으다) nectar all day long?" asked Maya.

Cassandra fetched(숨 등을 내쉬다, 가져오다) a deep sigh and gazed(응시하다) at the baby-bee seriously(심각하게) and sadly. She seemed to be thinking of her own toilsome(고달픈) life—toil(고생, 노고) from beginning to end, nothing but toil. Then she spoke in a changed voice, with a loving look in her eyes for the child.

"My dear little Maya, there will be other things in your life—the sunshine, lofty(우뚝 솟은, 아주 높은) green trees, flowery heaths(히스(진달랫과의 관목)), lakes of silver, rushing(빠르게 달리다), glistening(반짝 빛나다) waterways(수로), the heavens(하늘) blue and **radiant**(빛나는), and perhaps even human beings(human being 인간), the highest and most perfect(완전한) of Nature's creations(창작물). Because of all these glories(glory 찬란함, 장관) your work will become a joy. Just think—all that lies(놓여 있다) ahead of you, dear heart. You have good reason to be happy."

"I'm so glad," said Maya, "that's what I want to be."

Cassandra smiled kindly. In that instant—why, she did not know—she **conceive**d(품다) a peculiar(특이한) affection(애정) for the little bee, such as she could not recall(기억하다, 상기하다) ever having felt for any child-bee before. And that, probably, is how it came about((일이) 일어났다) that she told Maya more than a bee usually(보통) hears on the first day of its life. She gave her various(다양한) special bits of advice(충고), warned(경고하다) her against the dangers(위험) of the wicked(사악한) world, and named(이름을 말하다) the bees'(벌들의) most dangerous(위험한) enemies(적들). At the end she spoke long of human beings, and implanted(심다, 불어넣다) the first love for them in the child's heart and the germ(싹, 발아, 세균) of a great longing(동경) to know them.

"Be polite(공손한) and agreeable(다소곳한) to every insect(곤충) you meet," she said in conclusion(결론), "then you will learn more from them than I have told you to-day. But beware(조심해라) of the wasps(말벌) and hornets(장수말벌). The hornets are our most **formidable**(위협적인, 무서운) enemy, and the wickedest, and the wasps are a useless(쓸모 없는) tribe(부족) of thieves, without home or religion(종교). We are a stronger, more powerful nation, while they steal and **murder**(죽이다) wherever they can. You may use your sting (침) upon insects, to defend (방어하다) yourself and **inspire** (생기게 하다) respect, but if you **insert** (끼워 넣다) it in a warm-blooded (온혈의) animal, especially (특별히) a human being, you will die, because it will remain sticking (찌르다) in the skin and will break off. So do not sting warm-blooded creatures except in dire (절박한) need, and then do it without **flinch**ing (움찔하다) or fear of death. For it is to our courage (용감함) as well as our wisdom (지혜) that we bees owe (가지다, 얻다) the universal (우주의, 전부의) respect and esteem (존중) in which we are held. And now good-by, Maya dear. Good luck to you. Be faithful (충실한) to your people and your queen."

The little bee nodded yes, and returned her old monitor (충고자, 감시자)'s kiss and embrace (포옹). She went to bed in a **flutter** (두근거림, 흥분, 날갯짓) of secret joy and excitement and could scarcely fall asleep from curiosity (호기심). For the next day she was to know the great, wide world, the sun, the sky and the flowers.

Meanwhile the bee-city had quieted down (진정되었다). A large part of the younger bees had now left the kingdom (왕국) to found a new city; but for a long time the droning (drone 벌 등이 윙윙거리다, 단조로운 소리를 계속 내다) of the great swarm (떼, 무리) could be heard outside in the sunlight. It was not from **arrogance** (거만, 오만) or evil **intent** (의도) against the queen that these had **quit**ted (떠나다, 떠나가다, 그만두다); it was because the population (인구) had grown to such a size that there was no longer (더 이상 ~아니다) room (공간) for all the **inhabitant**s (거주자), and it was impossible to store (저장하다) a sufficient food-supply of honey to feed them all over the winter. You see, according to a government treaty of long standing, a large part of the honey gathered in summer had to be delivered up to human beings, who in return assured the welfare of the bee-state, provided for the peace and safety of the bees, and gave them shelter against the cold in winter.

"The sun has risen!"

The joyous call sounding in Maya's ears awoke her out of sleep the next morning. She jumped up and joined a lady working-bee.

"Delighted," said the lady cordially. "You may fly with me."

At the gate, where there was a great pushing and crowding, they were held up by the sentinels, one of whom gave Maya the password without which no bee was admitted into the city.

"Be sure to remember it," he said, "and good luck to you."

Outside the city gates, a flood of sunlight **assail**ed the little bee, a brilliance of green and gold, so rich and warm and **resplendent** that she had to close her eyes, not knowing what to say or do from sheer delight.

"Magnificent! It really is," she said to her companion. "Do we fly into that?"

"Right ahead!" answered the lady-bee.

Maya raised her little head and moved her pretty new wings. Suddenly she felt the flying-board on which she had been sitting sink down, while the ground seemed to be gliding away behind, and the large green domes of the tree-tops seemed to be coming toward her.

Her eyes sparkled, her heart rejoiced.

"I am flying," she cried. "It cannot be anything else. What I am doing must be flying. Why, it's splendid, perfectly splendid!"

"Yes, you're flying," said the lady-bee, who had difficulty in keeping up with the child. "Those are linden-trees, those toward which we are flying, the lindens in our castle park. You can always tell where our city is by those lindens. But you're flying so fast, Maya."

"Fast?" said Maya. "How can one fly fast enough? Oh, how sweet the sunshine smells!"

"No," replied her companion, who was rather out of breath, "it's not the sunshine, it's the flowers that smell.—But please, don't go so fast, else I'll drop behind. Besides, at this pace you won't observe things and be able to find your way back."

But little Maya **transport**ed(황홀하게 하다) by the sunshine and the joy of living, did not hear. She felt as though she were darting(질주하다) like an arrow through a green-shimmering(어른거리는) sea of light, to greater and greater splendor(호화, 장려). The bright flowers seemed to call to her, the still, sunlit(햇볕이 드는) distances(먼 곳) **lure**d(유혹하다) her on, and the blue sky blessed(축복하다) her joyous young flight(비행).

"Never again will it be as beautiful as it is to-day," she thought. "I can't turn back(등을 돌리다(거부하다)). I can't think of anything except the sun."

Beneath her the gay pictures kept changing(계속 변해왔다), the peaceful landscape(풍경) slid(slide (미끄러지다)의 과거) by slowly, in broad stretches(넓이, 범위).

"The sun must be all of gold," thought the baby-bee.

Coming to a large garden, which seemed to rest in blossoming(꽃피는) clouds of cherry(체리)-tree, hawthorn(산사나무), and lilacs(라일락), she let herself down to earth, dead-tired, and dropped(내리다) in a bed of red tulips, where she held on to one of the big flowers. With a great sigh of bliss(지복, 더 없는 기쁨) she pressed(누르다, 밀다) herself against the blossom-wall and looked up to the deep blue of the sky through the gleaming(반짝 빛나는) edges of the flowers.

"Oh, how beautiful it is out here in the great world,

a thousand times more beautiful than in the dark hive. I'll never go back there again to carry honey or make wax(밀랍). No, indeed, I'll never do that. I want to see and know the world in bloom(꽃). I am not like the other bees, my heart is meant for pleasure and surprises(놀라움), experiences(경험) and adventures. I will not be afraid of any dangers. Haven't I got strength(힘) and courage and a sting(침)?"

She laughed, bubbling(끓어오르는) over with delight, and took a deep draught(마시기, 한 모금) of nectar out of the flower of the tulip.

"Grand," she thought. "It's glorious(영광스러운) to be alive."

Ah, if little Maya had had an **inkling**(암시, 넌지시 비침) of the many dangers and hardships(곤경) that lay(놓여 있었다) ahead of her, she would certainly(틀림없이) have thought twice. But never dreaming of such things, she **stuck to**(충실했다, 끝까지 지켰다) her **resolve**(결심, 결의).

Soon tiredness(피곤함) overcame(압도했다) her, and she fell asleep. When she awoke, the sun was gone, twilight(황혼) lay upon the land. A bit of alarm(놀람), after all(결국). Maya's heart went a little faster.

Hesitatingly(주저하면서) she crept out of the flower, which was about to close up for the night, and hid(숨겼다) herself away under a leaf high up in the top of an old tree, where she went to sleep, thinking in the **utmost** (최고도의, 최대한) **confidence** (확신, 자신):

"I'm not afraid. I won't be afraid right at the very start. The sun is coming round again; that's certain; Cassandra said so. The thing to do is to go to sleep quietly and sleep well."

CHAPTER **02**

THE HOUSE OF THE ROSE

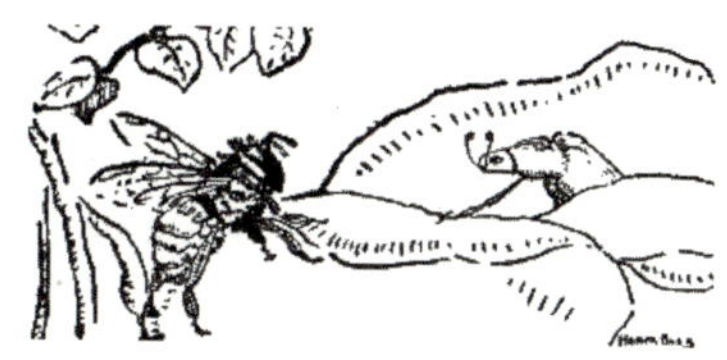

By the time Maya awoke, it was full daylight(낮). She felt a little chilly(추운) under her big green leaf, and stiff(뻣뻣한) in her limbs(사지(팔과 다리)), so that her first movements(움직임, 동작) were slow and **clumsy**(서투른). **Cling**ing to(~에 붙다) a vein((잎의)잎맥, 정맥) of the leaf she let her wings **quiver**(떨다) and **vibrate**(진동하다), to **limber**(유연하게 하다(up)) them up and shake off the dust; then she smoothed(손질하다, 부드럽게 하다) her fair hair, wiped her large eyes clean, and crept(기었다), **warily**(주의 깊게), down to the edge of the leaf, where she paused(잠시 멈추다) and looked around.

The glory and the glow(빛) of the morning sun were dazzling(빛나는, 눈부신). Though Maya's resting-place still lay in cool shadow, the leaves overhead(머리 위의) shone(빛났다) like green gold.

"Oh, you glorious world," thought the little bee.

Slowly, one by one, the experiences of the **previous** (전의) day came back to her—all the beauties (아름다움들) she had seen and all the risks (위험) she had run (위험을 무릅쓰다). She remained firm in her resolve not to return to the hive (벌집). To be sure, when she thought of Cassandra, her heart beat ((심장이) 뛰다) fast, though it was not very likely that Cassandra would ever find her.—No, no, to her there was no joy in forever having to fly in and out of the hive, carrying honey and making wax. This was clear, once and for all (단호하게). She wanted to be happy and free and enjoy life in her own way. Come what might, she would take the **consequence**s (결과).

Thus lightly (가볍게) thought Maya, the truth (진실) being that she had no real idea of the things that lay **in store for** (~을 위해 준비된(저장된)) her.

Afar (멀리서) off in the sunshine something glimmered (깜박깜박하다) red. A lurking (잠재해 있는; lurk 잠복하다) impatience (조급함) seized (붙잡다) the little bee. Moreover, she felt hungry. So, courageously (용기 있게), with a loud joyous buzz, she swung (swing (기세 좋게 움직이다, 휘두르다)의 과거) out of her hiding-place into the clear, glistening air and the warm sunlight, and made straight for (향해 갔다(for)) the red patch (조각, 작은 밭) that seemed to nod and beckon (손짓하여 부르다). When she drew near she smelled a perfume (향기, 향수) so sweet that it almost robbed (빼앗다) her of her senses, and she was hardly able to reach the large red flower. She let herself down on the outermost (가장 바깥쪽의) of its curved (굽은) petals (꽃잎) and clung to it tightly (단단히). At

the gentle tipping(끝) of the petal a shining silver **sphere**(구(球), 둥근 물체) almost as big as herself, came rolling toward her, transparent(투명한) and gleaming in all the colors of the rainbow. Maya was dreadfully frightened, yet fascinated(매혹 당한) too by the splendor of the cool silver sphere, which((sphere을 말함)) rolled by her, balanced(균형을 잡다) on the edge of the petal, leapt(leap (뛰다, 날쌔게 움직이다)의 과거) into the sunshine, and fell down in the grass. Oh, oh! The beautiful ball had shivered(박살나다, 떨다) into a score(20, 다수) of wee(작은) pearls(진주). Maya uttered(소리를 내다) a little cry of terror(공포). But the tiny round fragments(파편, 조각) made such a bright, lively glitter(광휘, 찬란함) in the grass, and ran down the blades(풀잎, 칼날) in such twinkling(순식간, 번쩍임), sparkling little drops((물)방울) like diamonds in the lamplight(등불), that she was reassured(안심하게 되었다).
(등불에 비추어진 다이아몬드처럼 반짝이는 물방울이 되어 순식간에 풀잎을 타고 내려갔다 그래서 그녀는 안심했다)

She turned towards the inside of the calix(꽃받침). A beetle, a little smaller than herself, with brown wing-sheaths(덮개, 외장) and a black breastplate(가슴받이), was sitting at the entrance(입구). He kept his place **unperturbed**(냉정한, 침착한), and looked at her seriously, though by no means(결코 ~아니다) unamiably(비우호적으로(amiable 상냥한, 친절한)). Maya bowed(인사하다) politely.

"Did the ball belong to(~의 것이다) you?" she asked, and receiving(receive 받다) no reply(대답) added(덧붙였다): "I am very sorry I threw it down."

"Do you mean the dewdrop(이슬방울)?" smiled the beetle, rather **superior**(으쓱하는, 거만한, 상위의). "You needn't worry about that. I had taken a drink already and my wife never drinks water, she has **kidney**(신장, 콩팥) trouble.—What are you doing here?"

"What is this wonderful flower?" asked Maya, not answering the beetle's question. "Would you be good enough to tell me its name?"

Remembering Cassandra's advice she was as polite as possible.

The beetle moved his shiny head in his **dorsal**(등의) plate(판), a thing he could do easily without the least discomfort(불편), as his head fitted(맞다) in perfectly and glided(미끄러지듯이 움직이다) back and forth without a click(찰칵 하는 소리).

"You seem to be only of yesterday(어제 태어난 것 같다(그만큼 모른다))?" he said, and laughed—not so very politely. Altogether there was something about him that struck(생각이 떠올랐다, 인상을 주었다) Maya as unrefined(세련되지 못한). (그에게 세련되지 못한 무언가가 있다고 마야에게 생각이 떠올랐다) The bees had more culture(교양) and better manners. Yet he seemed to be a good-natured fellow, because, seeing Maya's blush(얼굴이 붉어짐) of embarrassment(당황), he softened(누그러지다) to her childish(어린애 같은) ignorance(무지, 모름).

"It's a rose," he explained **indulgently**(너그럽게). "So now you know.—We moved in four days ago, and since we moved in, it has **flourish**ed(꽃 피우다, 번영하다) wonderfully under our care.—Won't you come in?"

Maya hesitated(망설이다), then **conquer**ed(정복하다) her misgivings(불안, 염려) and took a few steps forward. He pressed aside(옆으로 젖혔다) a bright petal, Maya entered, and she and the beetle walked beside each other through the narrow chambers (방) with their **subdued** (완화된, 억제된) light and **fragrant** (향기로운) walls.

"What a charming home!" exclaimed Maya, genuinely (진실로, 순수하게) taken (받아들여졌다) with the place. "The perfume is positively (확실히) intoxicating (취하게 하는)."

Maya's admiration (감탄) pleased the beetle.

"It takes wisdom to know where to live," he said, and smiled good-naturedly. "'Tell me where you live and I'll tell you what you're worth (가치 있는),' says an old **adage** (격언).—Would you like some nectar?"

"Oh," Maya burst out (갑자기 ~하다(냉큼 말했다)), "I'd love some."

The beetle nodded and disappeared behind one of the walls. Maya looked about. She was happy. She pressed her cheeks and little hands against the dainty (우아한) red hangings (걸려 있는 물건, 커튼) and took deep breaths (숨) of the delicious (매우 향긋한, 맛있는) perfume, in an ecstasy (황홀경) of delight at being permitted (허락 받다) to stop (방문하다, 들르다) in such a beautiful **dwelling** (주택, 주거).

"It certainly is a great joy to be alive," she thought. "And there's no **comparison** (비교) between the dingy (초라한, 더러운), crowded stories (같은 방들, 층들) in which the bees live and work and this house. The very quiet here is splendid."

Suddenly there was a loud sound of scolding (비난하다) behind the walls. It was the beetle growling (으르렁거리다) excitedly in great anger (화). He seemed to be hustling (hustle 난폭하게 밀다, 재촉하여 이동시키다) and pushing someone along roughly (거칠게), and Maya caught ((말을) 붙잡다, 들었다) the following (아래 사항), in a clear, piping (목소리가 피리처럼 날카로운) voice full of fright (겁) and **mortification** (억울, 분함, 굴욕).

"Of course, because I'm alone, you dare to lay hands on (붙잡다, 손대다) me. But wait and see what you get when I bring my **associates** (친구, 동료) along. You are a ruffian (악당, 불한당). Very well, I am going. But remember, I called you a ruffian. You'll never forget that."

The stranger's **emphatic** (강조된, 강경한) tone, so sharp and **vicious** (부도덕한, 타락한), frightened Maya dreadfully. In a few moments she heard the sound of someone running out.

The beetle returned and sullenly (언짢게, 시무룩하게) flung (툭 던졌다) down (아래로) some nectar.

"An outrage (무도한 행위)," he said. "You can't escape (피하다) those **vermin** (해충) anywhere. They don't allow (허락하다) you a moment's peace (평화)."

Maya was so hungry she forgot to thank him and took a mouthful of nectar and chewed (씹다), while the beetle wiped the perspiration (땀) from his forehead and slightly loosened (느슨하게 하다) his upper armor (갑옷) so as to (~하기 위해) catch his breath.

"Who was that?" mumbled Maya, with her mouth still full.

"Please empty(비우다) your mouth—finish chewing and swallowing(삼키다) your nectar. One can't understand a word you say."

Maya obeyed, but the excited(흥분한) owner(주인) of the house gave her no time to repeat her question.

"It was an ant," he burst out angrily. "Do those ants think we save and store(저장하다) up hour after hour only for them! The idea of going right into the pantry(식료품이나 식기를 두는 방) without a how-do-you-do or a by-your-leave(상대방의 양해를 구하기, 양해를 받지 않은데 대한 사과의 말)! It makes me furious(화나게). If I didn't realize(깨닫다) that the ill-mannered(예의 없는) creatures actually didn't know better(더 잘 알지 못했다(잘 알지 못할 만큼 철이 없다)), I wouldn't hesitate a second to call them—thieves(도둑들)!"

At this he suddenly remembered his own manners(예의범절).

"I beg your pardon(미안해요)," he said, turning to Maya, "I forgot to introduce(소개하다) myself. My name is Peter, of the family of rose-beetles."

"My name is Maya," said the little bee shyly. "I am delighted to make your **acquaintance**(앎, 사귐)." She looked at Peter closely(자세히); he was bowing repeatedly(되풀이하여), and spreading his **feeler**s(더듬이) like two little brown fans(부채). That pleased Maya immensely(몹시, 매우).

"You have the most fascinating (매혹적인) feelers," she said, "simply sweet..."

"Well, yes," observed Peter, flattered (우쭐해져; flatter 남에게 아첨하다, 남을 치켜세우다), "people do think a lot of them (그것들을 진정 많이 생각한다(그렇다고 생각한다)). Would you like to see the other side?"

"If I may."

The rose-beetle turned his fan-shaped (모양의) feelers to one side and let a ray (광선) of sunlight glide over them.

"Great, don't you think?" he asked.

"I shouldn't have thought anything like them possible," rejoined (재결합하다, 맞장구 치다) Maya. "My own feelers are very plain (평범한)."

"Well, yes," observed Peter, "to each his own. By way of **compensation** (보상) you certainly have beautiful eyes, and the color of your body, the gold of your body, is not to be sneezed at (얕볼 것이 아니다, 무시 못하다)."

Maya beamed (활짝 웃다). Peter was the first person to tell her she had any good looks. Life was great. She was happy as a lark, and helped (음식을 권하다) herself to some more nectar.

"An excellent **quality** (품질, 질) of honey," she remarked.

"Take some more," said Peter, rather amazed (놀란) by his little guest's appetite (식욕). "Rose-juice of the first **vintage** (수확기, ~년식(처음 수확한 것)). One has to be careful and not spoil (망치다) one's stomach (배, 위). There's some dew left, too, if you're thirsty."

"Thank you so much," said Maya. "I'd like to fly now, if you will permit (허락하다) me."

The rose-beetle laughed.

"Flying, always flying," he said. "It's in the blood (피) of you bees. I don't understand such a restless (가만히 있지 않는) way of living. There's some advantage (장점) in staying in one place, too, don't you think?"

Peter courteously (공손히) held the red curtain aside.

"I'll go as far as our **observation** (관측, 관찰 (전망대)) petal with you," he said. "It makes an excellent place to fly from."

"Oh, thank you," said Maya, "I can fly from anywhere."

"That's where you have the advantage over me," replied Peter. "I have some difficulty in unfolding (접은 것을 펴다) my lower wings." He shook her hand (그녀와 악수했다) and held the last curtain aside for her.

"Oh, the blue sky!" rejoiced (기뻐하다) Maya. "Good-by."

"So long," called Peter, remaining on the top petal to see Maya rise rapidly straight up to the sky in the golden sunlight and the clear, pure (맑은, 순수한) air of the morning. With a sigh he returned, **pensive** (생각에 잠긴, 애수 띤), to his cool rose-dwelling, for though it was still early he was feeling rather warm. He sang his morning song to himself, and it hummed in the red **sheen**(광택) of the petals and the **radiance**(빛남) of the spring day that slowly mounted(오르다) and spread(퍼지다) over the blossoming earth.

Gold and green are field and tree,
Warm in summer's glow;
All is bright and fair(날씨가 맑은, 좋은) to see
While the roses blow(꽃이 피다).
What or why the world may be
Who can guess or know?
All my world is glad and free
While the roses blow.
Brief, they say, my time of **glee**(환희);
With the roses I go;
Yes, but life is good to me
While the roses blow.

CHAPTER **03**

THE LAKE

"Dear me (이런, 아차)," thought Maya, after she had flown off, "oh, dear me, I forgot to ask Mr. Peter about human beings. A gentleman of his wide experience could certainly have told me about them. But perhaps I'll meet one myself to-day." Full of high spirits (기분, 정신) and in a happy mood (심정, 기분) of adventure, she let her bright eyes rove (방랑하다) over the wide landscape that lay spread out below in all its summer splendor.

She came to a large garden gleaming with a thousand colors. On her way she met many insects, who sang out greetings (인사), and wished her a pleasant journey and a good harvest (수확).—But every time she met a bee, her heart went pit-a-pat(두근두근). After all she felt a little **guilty**(죄의식의) to be idle, and was afraid of coming upon(우연히 만나다) acquaintances(아는 사람). Soon, however, she saw that the bees paid not the slightest(조금의) attention(주의, 집중) to her.

Then all of a sudden the world seemed to turn upside down. The heavens shone below her, in endless depths. At first she was dreadfully frightened; she thought she had flown too far up and lost her way in the sky. But presently she noticed that the trees were mirrored(비추다, 반영시키다) on the edge of the **terrestrial**(육지의) sky, and to her entrancement(무아의 경지, 황홀한 상태) she realized that she was looking at a great **serene**(고요한, 잔잔한) basin(물웅덩이, 분지, 대야) of water which lay blue and clear in the peaceful morning. She let herself down close to the surface. There was her image flying in reflection(반사), the lovely gold of her body shining at her from the water, her bright wings glittering like clear glass. And she observed that she held her little legs properly(적절히) against her body, as Cassandra had taught her to do.

"It's bliss to be flying over the surface(표면) of water like this. It is, really," she thought.

Big fish and little fish swam about in the clear element(성분, 요소(물을 말함)), or seemed to float(떠다니다) idly. Maya took good care not to go too close; she knew there was danger to bees from the race of fishes.

On the opposite shore she was attracted by the water-lilies and the rushes, the water-lilies with their large round leaves lying outspread on the water like green plates, and the rushes with their sun-warmed, reedy **stalk**s.

She picked out a leaf well-**conceal**ed under the tall blades of the rushes. It lay in almost total shade, except for two round spots like gold coins; the rushes swayed above in the full sunlight.

"Glorious," said the little bee, "perfectly glorious."

She began to tidy herself. Putting both arms up behind her head she pulled it forward as if to tear it off, but was careful not to pull too hard, just enough to **scrape** away the dust; then, with her little hind legs, she stroked and dragged down her wing-sheaths, which sprang back in position looking beautifully bright and **glossy**.

Just as she had completed her **toilet** a small steely blue-bottle came and alighted on the leaf beside her. He looked at her in surprise.

"What are you doing here on my leaf?" he demanded.

Maya was startled[놀란].

"Is there any **objection**[이의, 반대] to a person's just resting[쉬다] here a moment or two?"

Maya remembered Cassandra's telling her that the nation of bees commanded[관심 등을 모으다, 끌다] great respect in the insect world. Now she was going to see if it was true; she was going to see if she, Maya, could **compel**[억지로 만들다, 강요하다] respect. Nevertheless[그럼에도 불구하고] her heart beat a little faster[더 빨리] because her tone[어조, 말] had been very loud and **peremptory**[위압적인, 독단적인].

But actually the blue-bottle was frightened. He showed it plainly[분명히]. When he saw that Maya wasn't going to let anyone **lay down the law**[거만한 태도로 명령하다] to her he backed down[후퇴하다, 양보하다]. With a **surly**[퉁명스러운] buzz he swung himself on to a blade that curved[굽어 있다] above Maya's leaf, and said in a much politer[더 공손한] tone, talking down to her out of the sunshine:

"You ought to be working. As a bee you certainly ought. But if you want to rest, all right. I'll wait here."

"There are plenty[많음] of leaves," observed Maya.

"All rented[세 준, 빌려준]," said the blue-bottle. "Nowadays[요즈음] one is happy to be able to call a piece[조각] of ground one's own. If my **predecessor**[전임자] hadn't been snapped up[날름 삼키다, 덥석 물다] by a frog two days ago, I should still be without a proper place to live in. It's not very pleasant to have to hunt up[구하다, 사냥하다] a different lodging (숙소) every night. Not everyone has such a well-ordered (잘 정리된) state (국가) as you bees. But permit me to introduce myself. My name is Jack Christopher."

Maya was silent with terror, thinking how awful it must be to fall into the **clutch**es (손아귀, 붙잡음) of a frog.

"Are there many frogs in the lake?" she asked and drew (다가갔었다) to the very middle of the leaf so as not to (~하지 않기 위해) be seen from the water.

The blue-bottle laughed.

"You are giving yourself unnecessary (불필요한) trouble," he jeered (비웃다). "The frog can see you from below when the sun shines, because then the leaf is transparent. He sees you sitting on my leaf, perfectly."

Beset (포위 공격하다(여기서는 과거분사로 사용되었음. beset-beset-beset)) by the awful idea that maybe a big frog was squatting (웅크리다) right under her leaf staring at her with his bulging (부푼, 볼록한) hungry eyes, Maya was about to fly off when something dreadful happened, something for which she was totally unprepared (준비되지 않은). In the confusion (혼동) of the first moment she could not make out (이해하다, 알다) just exactly what was happening. She only heard a loud rustling (바스락 소리 나는) like the wind in dry leaves, then a singing whistle, a loud angry hunter's cry. And a fine, transparent shadow glided (미끄러져 가다) over her leaf. Now she saw—saw fully, and her heart stood still (정지한) in terror. A great, glittering dragon-fly(잠자리) had caught hold of poor Jack Christopher and held him tight in its large, **fang**s(송곳니), sharp as a knife. The blade of the rush bent(구부러졌다) low beneath their weight(무게). Maya could see them hovering(근처에 맴돌다) above her and also mirrored in the clear water below. Jack's screams(비명) tore(찢었다) her heart. Without thinking, she cried:

"Let the blue-bottle go, at once, whoever(~하는 사람은 누구나) you are. You have no right(권리) to interfere(방해하다) with people's habits(관습). You have no right to be so **arbitrary**(제멋대로의, 임의의)."

The dragon-fly **release**d(풀어주다) Jack from its fangs, but still held him fast with its arms, and turned its head toward Maya. She was fearfully(무섭게, 대단히) frightened by its large, **grave**(위험을 내포한, 장엄한) eyes and **vicious**(지독한, 잔인한, 악의가 있는) **pincer**s(집게발, 집게), but the glittering of its body and wings fascinated her. They flashed like glass and water and precious(귀중한) stones. The horrifying(오싹하게 하는) thing was its huge size. How could she have been so bold(대담한)? She was all a-tremble(떨림).

"Why, what's the matter, child?" The dragon-fly's tone, surprisingly, was quite friendly.

"Let him go," cried Maya, and tears came into her eyes. "His name is Jack Christopher."

The dragon-fly smiled.

"Why, little one?" it said, putting on an interested air, though most condescending.

Maya stammered helplessly:

"Oh, he's such a nice, elegant gentleman, and he's never done you any harm so far as I know."

The dragon-fly regarded Jack Christopher **contemplatively**.

"Yes, he is a dear little fellow," it replied tenderly and—bit Jack's head off.

Maya thought she was losing her senses. For a long time she couldn't utter a sound. In horror she listened to the munching and crunching above her as the body of Jack Christopher the blue-bottle was being **dismember**ed.

"Don't put on so," said the dragon-fly with its mouth full, chewing. "Your sensitiveness doesn't impress me. Are you bees any better? What do you do? Evidently you are very young still and haven't looked about in your own house. When the **massacre** of the drones takes place in the summer, the rest of the world is no less shocked and horrified, and I think with greater **justification**."

Maya asked:

"Have you finished up there?" She did not dare to

raise(올리다) her eyes.

"One leg still left," replied the dragon-fly.

"Do please swallow it. Then I'll answer you," cried Maya, who knew that the drones in the hive had to be killed off in the summer, and was provoked(분개시키다) by the dragon-fly's stupidity(어리석음). "But don't you dare to come a step closer. If you do I'll use my sting on you."

Little Maya had really lost her temper(화가 났다, 이성을 잃었다). It was the first time she had mentioned(말하다) her sting and the first time she felt glad that she possessed(가지다) the weapon(무기).

The dragon-fly threw her a wicked(악의 있는) glance. It had finished its meal and sat with its head slightly **duck**ed(고개 숙이다), fixing(노려보다, 고정시키다) Maya with its eyes and looking like a beast of prey about to **pounce**(덮치다). The little bee was quite calm now. Where she got her courage from she couldn't have told(알았다), but she was no longer afraid. She set up a very fine clear buzzing as she had once heard a sentinel(보초) do when a wasp came near the entrance(입구) of the hive.

The dragon-fly said slowly and threateningly(위협적으로):

"Dragon-flies live on the best terms((친한)사이) with the nation of bees."

"Very sensible(현명한, 어울리는) in them(그 사이에 관해 어울리게 행동하세요)," flashed(즉시 말하다) Maya.

"Do you mean to **insinuate**(넌지시 말하다) that I am afraid of(내가 너를(두려워해))

you—I of you?" With a jerk (갑작스런 움직임) the dragon-fly let go of the rush, which sprang back into its former (전의) position, and flew off with a whirr (윙윙 소리) and sparkle of its wings, straight down to the surface of the water, where it made a superb (훌륭한) appearance (외양, 모습) reflected in the mirror of the lake. You'd have thought there were two dragon-flies. Both moved their crystal (수정 같은, 수정) wings so swiftly (신속히) and finely (아름답게) that it seemed as though a brilliant sheen (광택, 광휘) of silver were streaming around them.

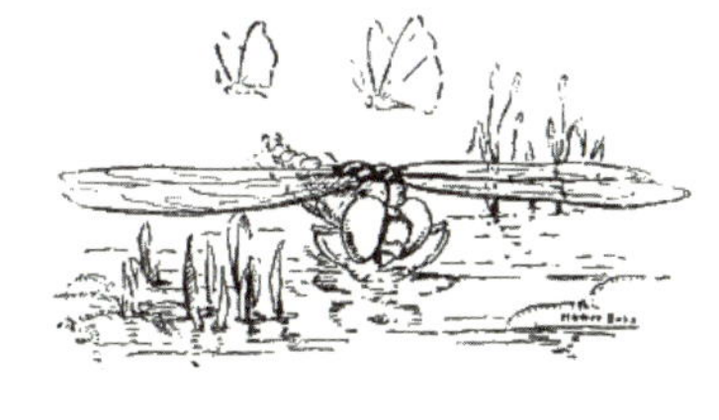

Maya quite forgot her grief over poor Jack Christopher and all sense of her own danger.

"How lovely! How lovely!" she cried enthusiastically (열광하여), clapping her hands.

"Do you mean me?" The drago-fly spoke in astonishment, but quickly added: "Yes, I must admit I am fairly presentable (외모가 단정한, 소개할만한). Yesterday I was flying along the brook (시내), and you should have heard some human beings who were lying on the bank (둑) **rave** (극찬하다, 헛소리하다) over me."

"Human beings!" exclaimed Maya. "Oh my, did you see human beings?"

"Of course," answered the dragon-fly. "But you'll

be very interested to know my name, I'm sure. My name is Loveydear, of the order (목(동식물의 분류 단계)) Odonata (잠자리목), of the family (과(동식물의 분류 단계)) Libellulidæ (잠자리과)."

"Oh, do tell me about human beings," implored Maya, after she had introduced herself.

The dragon-fly seemed won over (win over 설득시키다, 끌어들이다). She seated herself on the leaf beside Maya. And the little bee let her, knowing Miss Loveydear would be careful not to come too close.

"Have human beings a sting?" she asked.

"Good gracious, what would they do with a sting! No, they have worse weapons against us, and they are very dangerous. There isn't a soul (사람, 영혼) who isn't afraid of them, especially of the little ones whose two legs show (보이다)—the boys."

"Do they try to catch you?" asked Maya, breathless (숨찬) with excitement.

"Yes, can't you understand why?" Miss Loveydear glanced at her wings. "I have seldom (좀처럼 ~않다) met a human being who hasn't tried to catch me."

"But why?" asked Maya in a tremor.

"You see," said Miss Loveydear, with a modest (삼가는, 겸손한) smirk (능글맞은 웃음) and a **droop**ing (눈을 내리깔다, 머리 등을 숙이다), sidewise (비스듬한) glance, "there's something attractive(매력적인) about us dragon-flies. That's the only reason I know. Some members of our family who let themselves be caught went through(경험했다) the cruellest(가장 잔인한) tortures(고문) and finally died(죽었다)."

"Were they eaten up?"

"No, no, not exactly that," said Miss Loveydear comfortingly(달래는 듯이). "So far as is known, man does not feed(먹이를 먹다) on dragon-flies. But sometimes he has murderous(살인의) desires, a **lust**(욕망, 정욕) for killing, which will probably never be explained. You may not believe it, but cases have actually occurred of the so-called(소위) boy-men catching dragon-flies and pulling off their legs and wings for pure pleasure(즐거움). You doubt it, don't you?"

"Of course I doubt it," cried Maya indignantly(분개하여).

Miss Loveydear shrugged(어깨를 으쓱하다(냉소, 놀람 등의 표시로)) her glistening shoulders. Her face looked old with knowledge(앎, 지식).

"Oh," she said after a pause, grieving and pale(창백한), "if only one could speak of these things openly(솔직히). I had a brother who gave promise(전망, 약속) of a splendid future(미래), only, I'm sorry to say, he was a little **reckless**(무모한) and dreadfully curious. A boy once threw a net(그물) over him, a net fastened(고정시키다) to a long pole(장대).—Who would dream of a thing like that? Tell me. Would you?"

"No," said the little bee, "never. I should never have thought of such a thing."

The dragon-fly looked at her.

"A black cord(줄, 끈) was tied round his waist(허리) between his wings, so that he could fly, but not fly away, not escape. Each time my brother thought he had got his liberty(자유), he would be jerked(갑자기 당기다) back horribly within the boy's reach(닿음)."

Maya shook her head.

"You don't dare even think of it," she whispered.

"If a day passes when I don't think of it(그것을 생각하지 않고 하루라도 지나간다면)," said the dragon-fly, "I am sure to dream of it(그것에 관한 꿈이라도 분명히 꾸었어요). One misfortune(불행) followed another. My brother soon died." Miss Loveydear heaved(무거운 것을 내려놓다(들다), 한숨을 쉬다) a deep sigh.

"What did he die of?" asked Maya, in genuine(진짜의) **sympathy**(동정).

Miss Loveydear could not reply at once. Great tears **well**ed((우물처럼) 솟아나다) up and rolled down her cheeks.

"He was stuck(갇힌) in a pocket(호주머니)," she sobbed. "No one can stand(견디다, 참다) being stuck in a pocket."

"But what is a pocket?" Maya could hardly(거의 ~할 수 없다) take in(받아들이다) so many new and awful things all at once(동시에).

"A pocket," Miss Loveydear explained, "is a store-(보관방)

room that men have in their outer **hide** (가죽).—And what else do you think was in the pocket when my brother was stuck into it? Oh, the dreadful company (같이 있는 것, 동반) in which my poor brother had to draw (숨을 들이키다) his last breath! You'll never guess!"

"No," said Maya, all in a quiver (떨림), "no, I don't think I can.—Honey, perhaps?"

"Not likely," observed Miss Loveydear with an air of mingled (섞인) importance (중요함, 거만함) and distress (비통). "You'll seldom find honey in the pockets of human beings. I'll tell you.—A frog was in the pocket, and a pen-knife, and a carrot (당근). Well?"

"Horrible," whispered Maya.—"What is a pen-knife?"

"A pen-knife, in a way, is a human being's sting, an **artificial** (인공의) one. They are denied (deny 부정하다) a sting by nature, so they try to imitate (흉내내다) it.—The frog, thank goodness, was nearing (가까이 가다) his end (죽음, 끝). One eye was gone, one leg was broken, and his lower jaw (턱) was **dislocate**d (관절 등이 빠지다, 위치를 바꾸다). Yet, for all that (그럼에도 불구하고), the moment my brother was stuck in the pocket he hissed ((경멸, 비난, 공격의 감정으로) 시 하고 소리 내다) at him out of his crooked (구부러진) mouth:

"As soon as I am well, I will swallow you."

"With his remaining eye he glared (노려보다) at my brother,

and in the half-light (어스름, 박명(薄明)) of the prison (감옥) you can imagine what an effect (효과) the look (표정) he gave him must have had—fearful!—Then something even more horrible happened. The pocket was suddenly shaken (shake (흔들리다)의 과거분사), my brother was pressed (누르다) against the dying frog and his wings stuck (붙었다) to its cold, wet body. He went off (의식을 잃었다) in a faint (기절).—Oh, the misery (비참) of it! There are no words to describe (묘사하다) it."

"How did you find all this out?" Maya was so horrified (공포에 휩싸인) she could scarcely **frame** (마음에 품다, ~을 떠올리다, ~을 짜맞추다) the question.

"I'll tell you," replied Miss Loveydear. "After a while the boy got hungry and dug (뒤졌다, 팠다) into his pocket for the carrot. It was under my brother and the frog, and the boy threw them away first.—I heard my brother's cry for help, and found him lying beside the frog on the grass. I reached him only in time (시간에 맞게) to hear the whole story before he breathed (숨쉬다) his last. He put his arms round my neck and kissed me farewell (안녕). Then he died—bravely and without **complain**ing (불평하다), like a little hero. When his crushed (눌려 으깨진) wings had given their last quiver (떨림), I laid an oak leaf over his body and went to look for a sprig (잔가지, 어린 가지) of forget-me-nots (물망초) to put upon his grave (묘지, 무덤). 'Sleep well, my little brother,' I cried, and flew off in the quiet of the evening. I flew toward the two red suns, the one in the sky and the one in the lake. No one has ever felt as sad and solemn as I did then.—Have you ever had a sorrow in your life? Perhaps you'll tell me about it some other time."

"No," said Maya. "As a matter of fact, until now I have always been happy."

"You may thank your lucky stars," said Miss Loveydear with a note of disappointment in her voice.

Maya asked about the frog.

"Oh, him," said Miss Loveydear. "He, it is **presume**d, met with the end he deserved. The hard-heartedness of him, to frighten a dying person! When I found him on the grass beside my brother, he was trying to get away. But on account of his broken leg and one eye gone, all he could do was hop round in a circle and hop round in a circle. He looked too comical for words. 'The stork'll soon get ye,' I called to him as I flew away."

"Poor frog!" said little Maya.

"Poor frog! Poor frog indeed! That's going too far. Pitying a frog. The idea! To feel sorry for a frog is like clipping your own wings. You seem to have no principles."

"Perhaps. But it's hard for me to see any one

suffer(고통 받다)."

"Oh"—Miss Loveydear comforted(위로하다) her—"that's because you're so young. You'll learn to bear(견디다) it in time. Cheerio(안녕), my dear.—But I must be getting into the sunshine. It's pretty cold here. Good-by!"

A faint(희미한) rustle(바스락 소리) and the gleam(빛남) of a thousand colors, lovely pale colors like the glints(반짝거리는 빛) in running water and clear gems(보석).

Miss Loveydear swung through the green rushes(골풀) out over the surface of the water. Maya heard her singing in the sunshine. She stood and listened. It was a fine song, with something of the melancholy(우울한, 우울) sweetness(달콤함) of a folksong(민요), and it filled the little bee's heart with mingled happiness and sadness.

Softly flows the lovely stream
Touched by morning's rosy(장밋빛의) gleam(빛남)
Through the alders(오리나무) darted(화살처럼 날쌔게 움직이다),
Where the rushes bend and sway(흔들리다),
Where the water-lilies say
"We are golden-hearted!"
Warm the scent(향기, 냄새) the west-wind brings,
Bright the sun upon my wings,

Joy among the flowers!

Though my life may not be long,

Golden summer, take my song!

Thanks for perfect hours!

"Listen!" a white butterfly called to its friend. "Listen to the song of the dragon-fly." The light (산뜻한, 가벼운) creatures (생명체) rocked (흔들다(나비가 흔들흔들 움직이다)) close to Maya, and rocked away again into the radiant (빛나는) blue day. Then Maya also lifted (올리다) her wings, buzzed farewell to the silvery lake, and flew inland.

Maya lifted her wings, buzzed farewell to the lake, and flew inland

CHAPTER **04**

EFFIE AND BOBBIE

When Maya awoke the next morning in the corolla(화관(花冠), 꽃부리) of a blue canterbury(초롱꽃) bell, she heard a fine, faint rustling in the air and felt her blossom-bed(화단, 꽃밭) quiver as from a tiny, **furtive**(은밀한) tap-tapping(톡톡 두드리는 것). Through the open corolla came a damp(축축한) **whiff**(냄새 등의 한 번 풍기기) of grass and earth, and the air was quite chill. In some **apprehension**(염려, 걱정), she took a little **pollen**(꽃가루) from the yellow stamens(수술(꽃의)), scrupulously(꼼꼼하게) performed(행하다) her toilet(화장), then, warily(조심스럽게), picking her steps(걸음), ventured(용감하게 ~하다) to the outer edge of the drooping(숙인) blossom. It was raining! A fine cool rain was coming down with a light plash(철썩하는 소리), covering everything all round with millions of bright silver pearls(진주), which clung to(붙어 있었다) the leaves and flowers, rolled down the green paths of the blades of grass, and refreshed (상쾌하게 하다) the brown soil (흙).

What a change in the world! It was the first time in the child-bee's young life that she had seen rain. It filled (채우다) her with wonder; it delighted her. Yet she was a little troubled (불안한 듯한). She remembered Cassandra's warning (경고) never to fly abroad (바깥에, 외국에) in the rain. It must be difficult, she realized, to move your wings when the drops beat (때리다) them down. And the cold really hurt, and she missed (그리워하다) the quiet golden sunshine that gladdened (기쁘게 하다) the earth and made it a place free from all care.

It seemed to be very early still. The animal life in the grass was just beginning. From the **concealment** (숨음, 은닉) of her lofty (우뚝 솟은) bluebell (초롱꽃) Maya **command**ed (내려다보다) a splendid view of the social (사회의) life coming awake beneath (아래에). Watching it she forgot, for the moment, her anxiety (불안) and mounting (증가하는; mount 증대하다, 오르다) homesickness (향수병). It was too amusing (즐거운) for anything to be safe in a hiding-place, high up, and look down on the doings (하는 일) of the grass-dwellers (거주자, 주민) below.

Slowly, however, her thoughts went back—back to the home she had left, to the bee-state, and to the protection (보호, 방호) of its close **solidarity** (단결). There, on this rainy day, the bees would be sitting together, glad of the day of rest, doing a little construction(건설) here and there on the cells(벌집, 작게 구분된 작은 방), or feeding the **larva**(애벌레). Yet, on the whole(대체로), the hive was very quiet and Sunday-like when it rained. Only, sometimes messengers(전령) would fly out to see how the weather was and from what quarter(네 방위(동서남북) 중의 하나) the wind was blowing. The queen would go about her kingdom from story(층) to story, testing(살펴보다) things, **bestow**(주다)ing a word of praise or blame(책망, 비난), **lay**(알을 낳다)ing an egg here and there, and bringing happiness with her royal(왕의) presence((고귀한 사람의) 면전, 있음) wherever she went. She might pat(가볍게 두드리다) one of the younger bees on the head to show her **approval**(승인, 시인) of what it had already done, or she might ask it about its new experiences. How delighted a bee would be to catch a glance(흘깃 봄) or receive a gracious(자비로운) word from the queen!

Oh, thought Maya, how happy it made you to be able to count(포함시키다) yourself one in a **community**(공동체) like that, to feel that everybody respected you, and you had the powerful(강력한) protection of the state. Here, out in the world, lonely and **exposed**(노출된(위험 등에)), she ran great risks(위험) of her life. She was cold, too. And supposing the rain were to keep up(계속되다)! What would she do, how could she find something to eat? There was scarcely any honey-juice in the canterbury bell, and the pollen would soon **give out**(동나다, 바닥이 나다).

For the first time Maya realized how necessary (필요한) the sunshine is for a life of vagabondage (방랑, 방랑자). Hardly (거의 ~할 수 없는) anyone would set out on adventure, she thought, if it weren't for the sunshine. The very **recollection** (회상) of it was cheering, and she glowed (가슴이 벅차다, 빛나다) with secret pride (자부심) that she had had the daring (대담함, 용기) to start life **on her own hook** (스스로의 책임으로, 혼자 힘으로). The number of things she had already seen and experienced (경험하다)! More, ever so much more, than the other bees were likely to know in a whole lifetime. Experience was the most precious thing in life, worth (가치가 있는) any **sacrifice** (희생), she thought.

A troop (무리, 군대) of migrating (migrate 이동하다) ants were passing by, and singing as they marched (행진하다) through the cool forest of grass. They seemed to be in a hurry. Their crisp (힘찬, 파삭파삭한) morning song, in rhythm (리듬, 율동) with their march (행진), touched the little bee's heart with melancholy (우울함).

Few our days on earth shall be,
Fast the moments flit (휙 움직이다);
First-class (일류의) robbers (강도, 약탈자) such as we
Do not care a bit!

They were extraordinarily (몹시, 엄청나게) well armed (무장한) and looked **saucy** (건방진, 뻔뻔스러운), bold and dangerous.

The song died away under the leaves of the coltsfoot (colt (망아지)의 발 모양을 닮은 잎이 있는 식물). But some mischief (못된 짓) seemed to have been done there. A rough, hoarse (목이 쉰) voice sounded, and the small leaves of a young dandelion (민들레) were energetically (정력적으로) thrust (밀치다) aside. Maya saw a **corpulent** (뚱뚱한) blue beetle push its way out. It looked like a half-sphere (구) of dark metal (금속), shimmering with lights of blue and green and occasional (때때로의) black. It may have been two or even three times her size. Its hard sheath (덮개) looked as though nothing could destroy (파괴하다) it, and its deep voice positively (확실히) frightened you.

The song of the soldiers (병사), apparently (명백히), had roused (깨우다) him out of sleep. He was cross (시무룩한, 화난). His hair was still **rumple**d ((머리털 등을)헝클어뜨리다, 구기다), and he rubbed (비비다, 문질러 없애다) the sleep out of his cunning (간사한) little blue eyes.

"Make way (길을 만들어라(길을 비켜라)), I'm coming. Make way."

He seemed to think that people should step aside (옆으로 비키다) at the mere announcement (발표, 공고) of his approach (접근).

"Thank the Lord I'm not in his way," thought Maya, feeling very safe in her high, swaying nook (구석) of concealment. Nevertheless her heart went pit-a-pat (두근두근), and she withdrew (물러났다) a little deeper (더 깊은) into the flower-bell.

The beetle moved with a clumsy (꼴사나운) **lurch** (비틀거림, 갈짓자걸음, 배 등의 갑작스런 기울) through the wet grass, presenting (나타내다) a not exactly elegant appearance.

Directly [직접, 바로] under Maya's blossom was a **withered** [시든(wither 시들다)] leaf. Here he stopped, shoved [밀치다] the leaf aside, and made a step backward. Maya saw a hole in the ground.

"Well," she thought, all **agog** [~로 흥분한, ~하고 싶어 못 견디는] with curiosity [호기심], "the things there are in the world. I never thought of such a thing. Life's not long enough for all there is to see."

She kept very quiet. The only sound was the soft **pelt**ing [(비 등이) 내리치다, 두들기다] of the rain. Then she heard the beetle calling [소리치다] down [~아래로] the hole:

"If you want to go hunting with me, you'll have to make up your mind to get right up [바로 일어나다]. It's already bright daylight." He was feeling so very superior [우쭐한] for having waked up first that it was hard [확실한] for him to be pleasant [그가 기분 좋은 것은 확실하다].

A few moments passed before the answer came. Then Maya heard a thin, chirping [찍찍 울다] voice rise out of the hole.

"For goodness' sake, do [강조용법의 조동사] close the door up there. It's raining in."

The beetle obeyed. He stood in an expectant [기대하는] attitude [태도, 몸가짐], his head cocked [치켜 올리다] a little to one side, and squinted [가늘게 뜨다] through the crack [작은 틈새, 깨진 틈].

"Please hurry," he grumbled [불평하다].

Maya was tense [긴장한] with eagerness [열망, 갈망] to see what sort [종류] of a creature would come out of the hole. She crept so far out on the edge of the blossom that a drop of rain fell on her shoulder, and gave her a start(깜짝 놀람). She wiped(닦다) herself dry.

Below her the withered leaf heaved(무거운 것을 들어올리다); a brown insect crept out, slowly. Maya thought it was the queerest specimen(표본) she had ever seen. It had a **plump**(포동포동한) body, set(체격이 ~한) on extremely thin, slow-moving legs, and a fearfully thick head, with little upright feelers(더듬이). It looked flustered(초초한(fluster 혼란 시키다, 당황하게 하다)).

"Good morning, Effie dear." The beetle went slim(여윈) with politeness(공손함). He was all politeness, and his body seemed really slim. "How did you sleep? How did you sleep, my precious—my all?"

Effie took his hand rather stonily(무감동하게).

"It can't be, Bobbie," she said. "I can't go with you. We're creating(create 만들다) too much talk."

Poor Bobbie looked quite alarmed(놀란).

"I don't understand," he stammered. "I don't understand.—Is our new-found happiness to be wrecked(파괴하다, 배를 난파시키다) by such nonsense? Effie, think—think the thing over. What do you care(걱정하다) what people say? You have your hole, you can creep into it whenever you like, and if you go down far enough, you won't hear a syllable(음절)."

Effie smiled a sad, superior smile.

"Bobbie, you don't understand. I have my own views in the matter.—Besides, there's something else. You have been exceedingly **indelicate**. You took advantage of my ignorance. You let me think you were a rose-beetle and yesterday the snail told me you are a tumble-bug. A considerable difference! He saw you engaged in—well, doing something I don't care to mention. I'm sure you will now admit that I must take back my word."

Bobbie was stunned. When he recovered from the shock he burst out angrily:

"No, I don't understand. I can't understand. I want to be loved for myself, and not for my business."

"If only it weren't dung," said Effie offishly, "anything but dung, I shouldn't be so particular.—And please remember, I'm a young widow who lost her husband only three days ago under the most tragic circumstances—he was gobbled up by the shrewmouse—and it isn't proper for me to be **gad**ding about. A young widow should lead a life of complete **retirement**. So—goodby."

Pop into her hole went Effie, as though a puff of

wind had blown her away. Maya would never have thought it possible that anyone could dive into the ground as fast as that.

Effie was gone, and Bobbie stared in **blank** bewilderment down the empty dark opening, looking so utterly stupid that Maya had to laugh.

Finally he roused, and shook his small round head in angry distress. His feelers drooped dismally like two rain-soaked fans.

"People now-a-days no longer appreciate fineness of character and respectability," he sighed. "Effie is heartless. I didn't dare admit it to myself, but she is, she's absolutely heartless. But even if she hasn't got the right feelings, she ought to have the good sense to be my wife."

Maya saw the tears come to his eyes, and her heart was seized with pity.

But the next instant Bobbie stirred. He wiped the tears away and crept cautiously behind a small mound of earth, which his friend had probably shoveled out of her dwelling. A little flesh-colored earthworm was coming along through the grass. It had the queerest way of propelling itself, by first making itself long and thin, then short and thick. Its cylinder (원통, 원기둥) of a body **consisted of** (~로 구성되어 있다) nothing but delicate (미묘한) rings that pushed and groped (더듬으며 가다, (손으로) 더듬다) forward noiselessly (소리 없이).

Suddenly, startling (startle 놀라게 하다) Maya, Bobbie made one step out of his hiding-place, caught hold of the worm, bit it in two, and began calmly to eat the one half, heedless of (~에 상관없이) its desperate (필사적인) wriggling (꿈틀거림) or the wriggling of the other half in the grass. It was a tiny little worm.

"Patience (인내, 참음)," said Bobbie, "it will soon be over."

But while he chewed, his thoughts seemed to **revert** (되돌아가다) to Effie, his Effie, whom he had lost forever and aye (항상), and great tears rolled down his cheeks.

Maya pitied (가엾게 여겼다) him from the bottom of her heart.

"Dear me," she thought, "there certainly is a lot of sadness in the world."

At that moment she saw the half of the worm which Bobbie had set aside, making a hasty departure (출발).

"Did you ever see the like (이런 종류(것)를 보다니 믿을 수가 없어)!" she cried, surprised into such a loud tone that Bobbie looked around wondering (궁금해하다) where the sound had come from.

"Make way!" he called.

"But I'm not in your way," said Maya.

"Where are you then? You must be somewhere."

"Up here. Up above you. In the bluebell."

"I believe you, but I'm no grasshopper(메뚜기). I can't turn my head up far enough to see you. Why did you scream?"

"The half of the worm is running away."

"Yes," said Bobbie, looking after the retreating(후퇴하는) fraction(부분), "the creatures are very lively(활기찬).—I've lost my appetite." With that he threw away the **remnant**(나머지, 남은 부분) which he was still holding in his hand, and this worm portion(부분) also retreated(도망가다, 후퇴하다), in the other direction.

Maya was completely puzzled(어리둥절한). But Bobbie seemed to be familiar(익숙한) with this **peculiarity**(별남, 기묘함) of worms.

"Don't suppose that I always eat worms," he remarked. "You see, you don't find roses everywhere."

"Tell the little one at least which way its other half ran," cried Maya in great excitement.

Bobbie shook his head gravely.

"Those whom fate has rent(rend(찢다, 억지로 떼어놓다)의 과거분사) asunder(조각조각으로), let no man join together again," he observed.—"Who are you?"

"Maya, of the nation of bees."

"I'm glad to hear it. I have nothing against the bees.—Why are you sitting about? Bees don't usually sit about. Have you been sitting there long?"

"I slept here."

"Indeed!" There was a note of suspicion (의심) in Bobbie's voice. "I hope you slept well, very well. Did you just wake up?"

"Yes," said Maya, who had **shrewdly** (약삭빠르게) guessed that Bobbie would not like her having overheard (엿듣다) his conversation (대화) with Effie, the cricket, and did not want to hurt his feelings again.

Bobbie ran hither (여기로) and thither (저기로) trying to look up and see Maya.

"Wait," he said. "If I raise myself on my hind legs and lean (기대다) against that blade of grass I'll be able to see you, and you'll be able to look into my eyes. You want to, don't you?"

"Why, I do indeed. I'd like to very much."

Bobbie found a suitable (적합한) prop (받침대), the stem (줄기) of a buttercup (미나리아재비). The flower tipped (기울다) a little to one side so that Maya could see him perfectly as he raised himself on his hind legs and looked up at her. She thought he had a nice, dear, friendly face—but not so very young any more and cheeks rather too plump. He bowed, setting the buttercup a-rocking (흔들림), and introduced himself:

"Bobbie, of the family of rose-beetles."

Maya had to laugh to herself. She knew very well he was not a rose-beetle; he was a dung-beetle. But she passed the matter over in silence, not caring to **mortify** him.

"Don't you mind the rain?" she asked.

"Oh, no. I'm accustomed to the rain—from the roses, you know. It's usually raining there."

Maya thought to herself:

"After all I must punish him a little for his brazen lies. He's so frightfully **vain**."

"Bobbie," she said with a sly smile, "what sort of a hole is that one there, under the leaf?"

Bobbie started.

"A hole? A hole, did you say? There are very many holes round here. It's probably just an ordinary hole. You have no idea how many holes there are in the ground."

Bobbie had hardly uttered the last word when something dreadful happened. In his eagerness to appear indifferent he had lost his balance and **toppled** over. Maya heard a despairing shriek, and the next instant saw the beetle lying flat(납작하게) on his back in the grass, his arms and legs waving(wave 흔들다) pitifully(불쌍하게) in the air.

"I'm done for(끝장났다)," he wailed(울부짖다), "I'm done for. I can't get back on my feet again. I'll never be able to get back on my feet again. I'll die. I'll die in this position. Have you ever heard of a worse fate(운명)!"

He carried on(추태를 부렸다) so that he did not hear Maya trying to comfort(위로하다) him. And he kept making efforts(노력) to touch the ground with his feet. But each time he'd painfully(고통스럽게) get hold of a bit of earth, it would give way(무너지다, 굴복하다), and he'd fall over again on his high half-sphere of a back. The case looked really desperate(절망적인), and Maya was honestly(참으로) concerned(걱정한); he was already quite pale in the face and his cries were heart-rending(잡아 찢다).

"I can't stand it, I can't stand this position," he yelled. "At least(적어도) turn your head away. Don't torture(괴롭히다, 고문하다) a dying(죽어가는) man with your **inquisitive**(호기심 어린, 연구를 좋아하는) stares(응시).—If only I could reach a blade of grass, or the stem of the buttercup. You can't hold on to(~매달리다) the air. Nobody can do that. Nobody can hold on to the air."

Maya's heart was quivering with pity.

"Wait," she cried, "I'll try to turn you over. If I try very hard I am bound(~하게 되어 있는) to succeed. But Bobbie, Bobbie, dear man, don't yell (고함치다) like that. Listen to me. If I bend (굽히다) a blade of grass over and reach the tip of it to you, will you be able to use it and save yourself?"

Bobbie had no ears for her **suggestion** (제안). Frightened (겁먹은) out of his senses (그의 정신이 나가), he did nothing but kick and scream.

So little Maya, in spite of (~에도 불구하고) the rain, flew out of her cover (덮개) over to a slim green blade of grass beside Bobbie, and clung to it near the tip. It bent (굽혔다) under her weight and sank (가라앉혔다) directly above Bobbie's wriggling limbs. Maya gave a little cry of delight.

"Catch hold of it," she called.

Bobbie felt something tickle (간질이다) his face and quickly grabbed (붙잡다) at it, first with one hand, then with the other, and finally with his legs, which had splendid sharp claws, two each (각각에 두 개(의 날카로운 발톱)). Bit by bit (조금씩) he drew himself along the blade until he reached the base (밑동(풀의)), where it was thicker and stronger, and he was able to turn himself over on it.

He heaved a tremendous sigh of relief (안심).

"Good God!" he exclaimed. "That was awful. But for my presence of mind ((위기에서의) 침착, 냉정, 마음이 있음) I should have fallen a **victim** (희생자) to your talkativeness (수다)."

"Are you feeling better?" asked Maya.

Bobbie clutched (움켜잡다) his forehead.

“Thanks, thanks. When this dizziness passes, I’ll tell you all about it.”

But Maya never got the answer to her question. A field-sparrow came hopping through the grass in search of insects, and the little bee pressed herself close to the ground and kept very quiet until the bird had gone. When she looked around for Bobbie he had disappeared. So she too made off; for the rain had stopped and the day was clear and warm.

CHAPTER **05**

THE ACROBAT

Oh, what a day!

The dew had fallen early in the morning, and when the sun rose and cast(던지다) its slanting(비스듬한, 기울어진) beams(광선, 빛) across the forest of grass, there was such a sparkling(반짝이는) and glistening and gleaming(번쩍이다) that you didn't know what to say or do for sheer(순수한) ecstasy(황홀경), it was so beautiful, so beautiful!

(반짝이고 빛나고 번쩍여서 그 전적인 황홀경에 뭐라고 말해야 할지 무엇을 해야 할지 모르겠다(such~that))

The moment Maya awoke, glad sounds greeted(맞이하다) her from all round. Some came out of the trees, from the throats(목구멍) of the birds, the dreaded(두려운) creatures who could yet produce(낳다) such **exquisite**(아주 아름다운) song; other happy calls came out of the air, from flying insects, or out of the grass and the bushes, from bugs and flies, big ones and little ones.

Maya had made it very comfortable for herself in a hole in a tree. It was safe and dry, and stayed warm the greater part of the night because the sun shone on the entrance all day long. Once, early in the morning, she had heard a woodpecker rat-a-tat-tatting (쾅쾅 두드리는 소리) on the bark (껍질) of the trunk (나무의 원줄기), and had lost no time (즉시 ~했다(시간을 잃지 않았으니)) getting away (도망가다). The drumming (두드리는 소리) of a woodpecker is as terrifying to a little insect in the bark of a tree as the breaking open of our shutters (셔터, 덧문) by a burglar (강도) would be to us. But at night she was safe in her lofty nook. At night no creatures came **pry**ing (떼어내다, 엿보다).

She had **seal**ed (봉하다, 막다) up part of the entrance with wax, leaving just space enough to slip (살짝 가다) in and out; and in a cranny (갈라진 틈) in the back of the hole, where it was dark and cool, she had stored (저장하다) a little honey against rainy (비오는) days.

This morning she swung (기세 좋게 움직였다) herself out into the sunshine with a cry of delight (기쁨), all **anticipation** (기대) as to what the fresh, lovely day might bring. She sailed (나아가다) straight through the golden air, looking like a brisk (팔팔한, 활발한) dot (점) driven (drive(바람이 ~을 떠밀다)의 과거분사) by the wind.

"I am going to meet a human being to-day," she cried. "I feel sure I am. On days like this human beings must certainly be out in the open air enjoying nature."

Never had she met so many insects (그토록 많은 곤충들을 만난 적이 없었다(가장 많이 만났다)). There was a coming and going and all sorts of doings; the air was alive with a humming and a laughing and glad little cries. You had to join in, you just had to join in.

After a while Maya let herself down into a forest of grass, where all sorts of plants (식물) and flowers were growing. The highest were the white **tufts** ((머리털이나 실 등의) 다발) of yarrow (서양가새풀) and butterfly-weed—the flaming (불꽃같은) milkweed (흰 액을 분비하는 식물의 총칭) that drew you like a **magnet** (자석). She took a **sip** (한 모금, 홀짝 마시기) of nectar from some clover and was about to fly off again when she saw a perfect droll (어릿광대, 우스운 모양) of a beast perched ((높은 곳에)앉아 있다) on a blade of grass curving above her flower. She was thoroughly scared—he was such a lean (마른) green monster—but then her interest was tremendously (엄청나게) aroused (관심 등을 유발하다), and she remained sitting still, as though rooted (뿌리박다) to the spot, and stared straight at him.

At first glance you'd have thought he had horns (뿔). Looking closer you saw it was his oddly (기묘하게) **protuberant** (돌출한) forehead that gave this impression (인상). Two long, long feelers fine (가는) as the finest thread (실) grew out of his brows (이마), and his body was the slimmest imaginable (상상할 수 있는), and green all over, even to his eyes. He had dainty forelegs and thin, **inconspicuous** (주의를 끌지 않는) wings that couldn't be very practical (실제적인),

Maya thought. Oddest of all were his great hindlegs(뒷다리), which stuck up over his body like two jointed(마디가 있는) **stilt**s(죽마). His sly, saucy expression(표정) was **contradict**ed(반박하다, 이의를 제기하다) by the look of astonishment(놀라움) in his eyes(그의 교활하고 거만한 표정은 놀라움에 의해 없어지지 않았다), and you couldn't say there was any meanness(비열함) in his eyes either. No, rather a lot of good humor.

"Well, mademoiselle(아가씨, …양(孃))," he said to Maya, evidently(분명히) annoyed(불쾌하게 여기다) by her surprised expression, "never seen a grasshopper before? Or are you laying eggs?"

"The idea!(그 아이디어-말도 안 되는 생각 말아요)" cried Maya in shocked accents(어조, 말투). "It wouldn't occur to me. Even if I could, I wouldn't. It would be **usurp**ing(강탈하다, 불법 사용하다) the sacred(신성한) duties of our queen. I wouldn't do such a foolish thing."

The grasshopper ducked his head and made such a funny face that Maya had to laugh out loud in spite of her **chagrin**(분함).

"Mademoiselle," he began, then had to laugh himself, and said: "You're a case(문제아)! You're a case!"

The fellow's behavior(행동) made Maya impatient(초조하게).

"Why do you laugh?" she asked in a not altogether friendly tone. "You can't be serious expecting me to lay eggs, especially out here on the grass."

There was a snap(딱 하는(소리)). "Hoppety-hop(폴짝)," said the grasshopper, and was gone.

Maya was utterly non-plussed (어찌할 바를 모르게 하다). Without the help of his wings he had swung himself up in the air in a tremendous (엄청난) curve (곡선). Foolhardiness (무모함) **border**ing (경계선을 이루다, 이웃하다, 가깝다) on madness (미침), she thought.

But there he was again. From where, she couldn't tell, but there he was, beside her, on a leaf of her clover.

He looked her up and down, all round, before and behind.

"No," he said then, pertly (주제넘게), "you certainly can't lay eggs. You're not **equip**ped (필요한 것을 갖추다) for it. You haven't got a borer (구멍을 뚫는 것(구멍을 뚫어 그곳에 알을 낳는다))."

"What—borer?" Maya covered herself with her wings and turned so that (그래서) the stranger could see nothing but her face.

"Borer, that's what I said.—Don't fall off your base (근거지, 기지), mademoiselle.—You're a wasp, aren't you?"

To be called a wasp! Nothing worse could happen to little Maya.

"I never!" she cried.

"Hoppety-hop," answered he, and was off again.

"The fellow makes me nervous (짜증나게, 신경 쓰이게)," she thought, and decided to fly away. She couldn't remember ever having been so insulted in her life. What a disgrace to be mistaken for a wasp, one of those useless wasps, those tramps, those common thieves! It really was **infuriating**.

But there he was again!

"Mademoiselle," he called and turned round part way, so that his long hindlegs looked like the hands of a clock standing at five minutes before half-past seven, "mademoiselle, you must excuse me for interrupting our conversation now and then. But suddenly I'm seized. I must hop. I can't help it, I must hop, no matter where. Can't you hop, too?"

He smiled a smile that drew his mouth from ear to ear. Maya couldn't keep from laughing.

"Can you?" said the grasshopper, and nodded encouragingly.

"Who are you?" asked Maya. "You're terribly exciting."

"Why, everybody knows who I am," said the green oddity, and grinned almost beyond the limits of his jaws.

Maya never could make out whether he spoke in fun or in earnest.

"I'm a stranger in these parts," she replied pleasantly, "else I'm sure I'd know you.—But please note that I belong to the family of bees, and am positively not a wasp."

"My goodness," said the grasshopper, "one and the same thing (같은 것이다(말벌이나 일벌이나 그게 그거다))."

Maya couldn't utter a sound, she was so excited (흥분한).

"You're uneducated (무식한, 교육을 받지 않은)," she burst out at length (마침내). "Take a good look at a wasp once."

"Why should I?" answered the green one. "What good would it do if I observed (보다, 관찰하다) differences (차이) that exist (존재하다) only in people's imagination (상상)? You, a bee, fly round in the air, sting (침을 쏘다) everything you come across (만나다), and can't hop (깡충 뛰다). Exactly the same with a wasp. So where's the difference? Hoppety-hop!" And he was gone.

"But now I am going to fly away," thought Maya.

There he was again.

"Mademoiselle," he called, "there's going to be a hopping-match (시합) to-morrow. It will be held in the Reverend (목사) Sinpeck's garden. Would you care to have a **complimentary** (무료의, 칭찬하는) ticket and watch the games? My old woman (마누라, 부인) has two left over. She'll trade (교환하다) you one for a **compliment** (찬사, 아첨(말만 잘하면 준다는 말)). I expect to break the record."

"I'm not interested in hopping **acrobatics** (곡예)," said Maya in some disgust (혐오, 반감). "A person who flies has higher (더 고상한, 더 높은)

(나는 사람(벌 같이)은 더 고상한데 관심이 있다)

interests(관심, 흥미)."

The grasshopper grinned a grin you could almost hear.

"Don't think too highly of yourself(당신을 높게 평가하지 마세요), my dear young lady. Most creatures in this world can fly, but only a very, very few can hop. You don't understand other people's interests. You have no vision. Even human beings would like a high elegant(우아한) hop. The other day I saw the Reverend Sinpeck hop a yard up into the air to impress(감명을 주다) a little snake that slid(slide (미끄러지듯 움직이다)의 과거) across his road. His **contempt**(경멸) for anything that couldn't hop was so great that he threw away his pipe((담배)파이프). And reverends, you know, cannot live without their pipes. I have known grasshoppers—members of my own family—who could hop to a height(높이) three hundred times their length(길이). Now you're impressed. You haven't a word to say. And you're inwardly(마음 속 깊이) regretting(후회하다) the remarks(말) you made and the remarks you intended(~하려 하다) to make. Three hundred times their own length! Just imagine. Even the elephant, the largest animal in the world, can't hop as high as that. Well? You're not saying anything. Didn't I tell you you wouldn't have anything to say?"

"But how can I say anything if you don't give me

a chance?"

"All right, then, talk," said the grasshopper pleasantly. "Hoppety-hop." He was gone.

Maya had to laugh in spite of her **irritation**(안달, 짜증).

The fellow had certainly(분명히) **furnish**(제공하다)ed her with a strange experience. Buffoon(익살꾼) though he was, still she had to admire his wide information(정보) and worldly(세상의) wisdom(지혜); and though she could not agree(동의하다) with his views(견해) of hopping, she was amazed by all the new things he had taught her in their brief(짧은) conversation. If he had been more reliable(신뢰할 수 있는) she would have been only too glad to ask him questions about a number of different things. It occurred(생각 등이 떠오르다, 일어나다) to her that often people who are least equipped to **profit**(도움이 되다) by experiences are the very ones who have them.
(경험에 의해 도움이 되는 것을 전혀 갖추지 않은 사람들이 때때로 그것들(경험들)을 가진 바로 그 사람들이다)

He knew the names of human beings. Did he, then, understand their language(말)? If he came back, she'd ask him. And she'd also ask him what he thought of trying to go near a human being or of entering a human being's house.

"Mademoiselle!" A blade of grass beside Maya

was set swaying(흔들리다).

"Goodness gracious! Where do you keep coming from(어디로부터 계속 오느냐)?"

"The surroundings(주위, 환경)."

"But do tell, do you hop out into the world just so, without knowing where you mean(마음먹다, 작정하다) to land?"

"Of course(당연하죠(어디로 갈지 모르고 뛰는 것이)). Why not(왜 아니겠어요)? Can you read the future? No one can. Only the tree-toad(두꺼비), but he never tells."

"The things you know! Wonderful, simply wonderful!—Do you understand the language of human beings?"

"That's a difficult question to answer, mademoiselle, because it hasn't been proved(증명하다) as yet whether human beings have a language. Sometimes they utter(소리를 내다) sounds by which they seem to reach(이르다, 도달하다) an understanding with each other—but such awful sounds! So unmelodious(가락이 없는)! Like nothing else in nature that I know of. However, there's one thing you must allow them: they do seem to try to make their voices pleasanter(더 즐겁게). Once I saw two boys take a blade of grass between their thumbs(엄지) and blow on it. The result was a whistle(휘파람) which may be **compare**d(비교하다, 견주다) with the chirping of a cricket, though far inferior(열등한, 하위의) in quality of tone, far inferior. However, human beings make an honest effort.—Is there anything else you'd like to ask? I know a thing or two."

He grinned his almost-audible (들을 수 있는) grin.

But the next time he hopped off, Maya waited for him in vain (보람없이, 헛된). She looked about in the grass and the flowers; he was nowhere to be seen.

CHAPTER 06

PUCK

Maya, drowsy(졸린) with the noonday heat, flew leisurely(느긋하게) past the glare(번쩍이는 빛) on the bushes(관목) in the garden, into the cool, broad(넓은)-leaved shelter(대피소, 피난처) of a great chestnut-tree.

On the trodden(tread (밟다)의 과거분사) sward(풀밭, 잔디) in the shade(그늘) under the tree stood chairs and tables, evidently for an out-door meal(식사). A short distance away gleamed(빛나다) the red-tiled(타일을 붙이다) roof of a peasant(농부)'s cottage, with thin blue columns(기둥) of smoke curling up(소용돌이치며 올라가다) from the chimneys(굴뚝).

Now at last, thought Maya, she was bound(~하게 되어 있는) to see a human being. Had she not reached the very heart of his **realm**(영역, 국토)? The tree must be his **property**(재산, 자산), and the curious wooden **contrivance**(고안품)s in the shade below must be-

long to his hive(벌집).
(그의 벌집에 속하다-그의 집에 속하다)

Something buzzed; a fly alighted on the leaf beside her. It ran up and down the green veining(잎맥) in little jerks(갑작스런 움직임). You couldn't see its legs move, and it seemed to be sliding about excitedly. Then it flew from one finger(손가락 모양) of the broad leaf to another, but so quickly and unexpectedly that you might have thought it hadn't flown but hopped. Evidently it was looking for the most comfortable place on the leaf. Every now and then(때때로), in the suddennest(갑작스러운) way, it would swing itself up in the air a short space(거리, 공간) and buzz(앵앵대다) **vehemently**(격렬히), as though something dreadfully **untoward**(온당치 못한) had occurred, or as though it were **animate**(활발하게 하다, 생명을 주다)d by some tremendous purpose(목적). Then it would drop back to the leaf, as if nothing had happened, and resume(다시 계속하다) its jerky racing up and down. Lastly, it would sit quite still, like a rigid(굳은) image.

Maya watched its antics(괴상한 짓거리) in the sunshine, then approached it and said politely:

"How do you do? Welcome to my leaf. You are a fly(파리), are you not?"

"What else do you take me for?" said the little one. "My name is Puck. I am very busy. Do you want to drive me away?"

"Why, not at all. I am glad to make your acquaintance(앎)."

"I believe you," was all Puck said, and with that he tried to pull his head off.

"Mercy(저런, 어머나, 자비)!" cried Maya.

"I must do this. You don't understand. It's something you know nothing about," Puck rejoined(~이라고 대답하다, 다시 가입하다) calmly, and slid his legs over his wings till they curved round the tip of his body(몸통 끝까지 날개가 굽어 펴질 때까지). "I'm more than a fly," he added with some pride. "I'm a housefly. I flew out here for the fresh(신선한) air."

"How interesting!" exclaimed Maya gleefully(매우 기뻐하며). "Then you must know all about human beings."

"As well as the pockets of my trousers(바지)," Puck threw out(던졌다(말을 내뱉었다)) disdainfully(아무렇게나, 오만하게). "I sit on them every day. Didn't you know that? I thought you bees were so clever. You pretend(~인 체하다) to be at any rate(하여튼)."

"My name is Maya," said the little bee rather shyly. Where the other insects got their self-assurance(자기 과신), **to say nothing of**(~은 말할 것도 없이) their **insolence**(오만, 거만, 무례), she couldn't understand.

"Thanks for the information. Whatever your name, you're a simpleton(얼간이, 바보)."

Puck sat there tilted(공격하다, 찌르다, 기울다) like a cannon in position to be fired off(발사하다), his head and breast thrust(내밀다, 찌르다) upward, the hind(뒤) tip of his body resting on the leaf. Suddenly he ducked(고개를 숙이다) his head and squatted(웅크리다) down, so that he looked as if he had no legs.

"You've got to watch out(조심하다) and be careful(사람에게 앉을 때)," he said. "That's the most important thing of all."

But an angry wave of **resentment**(분개, 적의) was surging(surge 굽이치다, 밀려오다) in little Maya. The insult(모욕) Puck had offered her was too much. Without really knowing what made her do it, she pounced(덤벼들다) on him quick as lightning(번개), caught him by the collar(목덜미) and held him tight.

"I will teach you to be polite to a bee," she cried.

Puck set up an awful howl.

"Don't sting me," he screamed. "It's the only thing you can do, but it's killing. Please remove(옮기다, 치우다) the back of your body. That's where your sting is. And let me go, please let me go, if you possibly can. I'll do anything you say. Can't you understand a joke, a mere joke? Everybody knows that you bees are the most respected(존경 받는) of all insects, and the most powerful, and the most numerous(수가 많은). Only don't kill me, please don't. There won't be any bringing me back to life. Good God! No one appreciates my humor!"

"Very well," said Maya with a touch of contempt in her heart, "I'll let you live on condition that you tell me everything you know about human beings."

"Gladly," cried Puck. "I'd have told you anyhow. But please let me go now."

Maya released him. She had stopped caring. Her respect for the fly and any confidence she might have had in him were gone. Of what value could the experiences of so low, so **vulgar** a creature be to serious-minded people? She would have to find out about human beings for herself.

The lesson, however, had not been wasted. Puck was much more **endurable** now. Scolding and growling he set himself to rights. He smoothed down his feelers and wings and the **minute** hairs on his black body—which were fearfully rumpled; for the girl-bee had laid on good and hard—and concluded the operation by running his **proboscis** in and out several times—something new to Maya.

"Out of joint, completely out of joint!" he muttered in a pained tone. "Comes of your excited way of doing things. Look. See for yourself. The sucking-disk at the end of my proboscis looks like a twisted pewter(백랍) plate(쟁반)."

"Have you a sucking-disk?" asked Maya.

"Goodness gracious, of course!—Now tell me. What do you want to know about human beings?—Never mind about my proboscis being out of joint. It'll be all right.—I think I had best tell you a few things from my own life. You see, I grew up among human beings, so you'll hear just what you want to know."

"You grew up among human beings?"

"Of course. It was in the corner of their room that my mother laid the egg from which I came. I made my first attempts(시도) to walk on their window-shades(커튼, 가리개), and I tested the strength of my wings by flying from Schiller to Goethe."

"What are Schiller and Goethe?"

"**Statue**(동상)s," explained Puck, very superior, "statues of two men who seem to have **distinguish**(유명하게 하다, 구별하다)ed themselves. They stand under the mirror, one on the right hand(오른쪽) and one on the left hand, and nobody pays any attention(관심, 주의) to them."

"What's a mirror? And why do the statues stand under the mirror?"

"A mirror is good for seeing your belly(배) when you crawl on it. It's very amusing. When human beings go up to a mirror, they either put their hands up to their hair, or pull at their beards. When they are alone, they smile into the mirror, but if somebody else is in the room they look very serious. What the purpose of it is, I could never make out. Seems to be some useless game of theirs. I myself, when I was still a child, suffered(고통 받다) a good deal from the mirror. I'd fly into it and of course be thrown back violently(격렬히)."

Maya plied(ply 끈질기게 묻다, 부지런히 하다) Puck with more questions about the mirror, which he found very difficult to answer.

"Here," he said at last, "you've certainly flown over the smooth surface of water, haven't you? Well, a mirror is something like it, only hard and upright(똑바로 선)."

The little fly, seeing that Maya listened most respectfully and attentively(집중하여) to the tale of his experiences, became a good deal pleasanter in his manners. And as for Maya's opinion of Puck, although she didn't believe everything he told her, still she was sorry she had thought so slightingly(업신여기는, 무시하는) of him earlier in their meeting.

"Often people are far more sensible(현명한) than we take them to be at first," she told herself.

Puck went on with his story.

"It took a long time for me to get to understand their language. Now at last I know what they want. It isn't much, because they usually say the same thing every day."

"I can scarcely believe it," said Maya. "Why, they have so many interests, and think so many things, and do so many things. Cassandra told me that they build cities so big that you can't fly round them in one day, towers(탑) as high as the **nuptial**(결혼식의, 결혼식) flight of our queen, houses that float(둥둥 떠다니다) on the water, and houses that glide across the country on two narrow silver paths(철도를 말함) and go faster than birds."

"Wait a moment!" said Puck energetically. "Who is Cassandra? Who is she, if I may make so bold as to ask? Well?"

"Oh, she was my teacher."

"Teacher!" repeated Puck contemptuously(경멸적으로). "Probably also a bee. Who but(제외하고) a bee would overestimate(과대평가하다) human beings like that? Your Miss Cassandra, or whatever her name is, doesn't know her history(역사). Those cities and towers and other human devices(장치, 장비) you speak of are none of them any good to us. Who would take such an

impractical [비실용적인, 비현실적인] view of the world as you do? If you don't accept [받아들이다] the **premise** [전제] that the earth is **dominate**d [지배하다, 복종하다] by the flies, that the flies are the most widespread [널리 퍼진] and most important race [종] on earth, you'll scarcely get a real knowledge [지식, 앎] of the world."

Puck took a few excited zigzag [지그재그] turns [방향전환] on the leaf and pulled at his head, to Maya's intense concern [걱정(마야가 심하게 걱정되게끔)]. However, the little bee had observed by this time that there wasn't much sense to be got out of his head any way.

"Do you know how you can tell I am right?" asked Puck, rubbing his hands together as if to tie [묶다] them in a knot [매듭]. "Count the number of people and the number of flies in any room. The result will surprise you."

"You may be right. But that's not the point [중요한 사항, 요점]."

"Do you think I was born this year?" Puck demanded [다그쳐 묻다, 요구하다] all of a sudden.

"I don't know."

"I passed through a winter," Puck announced, all pride. "My experiences date back [시기를 거슬러 가다] to the ice age [빙하기]. In a sense [어떤 의미에서] they [경험들] take me through the ice age. That's why I'm here—I'm here to **recuperate** [회복하다, 재기하다]."

"Whatever else you may be, you certainly are spunky(원기 왕성한)," remarked Maya.

"I should say so(그렇게 분명히 말해야 한다(그럼요))," exclaimed Puck, and made an airy(경쾌한) leap out into the sunshine. "The flies are the boldest race in creation(창조). We never run away unless it is better to run away, and then we always come back.—Have you ever sat on a human being?"

"No," said Maya, looking at the fly distrustfully(미심쩍은 듯, 믿지 못하다는 듯) out of the corner of her eye(곁눈질로). She still didn't know quite what to make of him. "No, I'm not interested in sitting on human beings."

"Ah, dear child, that's because you don't know what it is. If ever you had seen the fun I have with the man at home, you'd turn green with envy(부러움). I'll tell you.—In my room there lives an elderly man who cherishes(귀여워하다) the color of his nose by means of(~에 의해) a peculiar(특이한) drink, which he keeps hidden in the corner cupboard(찬장). It has a sweet, intoxicating(취하게 하는) smell. When he goes to get it he smiles, and his eyes grow small. He takes a little glass, and he looks up to the ceiling while he drinks, to see if I am there. I nod down to him, and he passes his hand over his fore-head, nose and mouth to show me where I am to sit later on. Then he blinks(눈을 깜박이다), and opens his mouth as wide as he can, and pulls down the shade (가리개, 커튼) to keep (막다, 방지하다(from)) the afternoon sun from bothering (귀찮게 하다) us. Finally he lays himself down on a something called a sofa, and in a short while begins to make dull snuffling (코를 킁킁거리는(자면서)) sounds. I suppose he thinks the sounds are beautiful. We'll talk about them some other time. They are man's slumber (잠) song. For me they are the sign that I am to come down. The first thing I do is to take my portion (음식의 1인분, 부분) from the glass, which he left for me. There's something tremendously stimulating (자극하는) about a drop like that. I understand human beings. Then I fly over and take my place on the forehead of the sleeping man. The forehead lies between the nose and the hair and serves (사용되다, 봉사하다) for thinking. You can tell it does from the long **furrow**s (고랑, 밭고랑) that go from right to left. They must move whenever a man thinks if something worth while (가치 있는) is to result (결과로 생기다) from his thinking. The forehead also shows if human beings are annoyed (화가 난). But then the folds (주름) run up and down, and a round **cavity** (구멍, 공동) forms over the nose. As soon as I settle on his forehead and begin to run to and fro (이리저리로) in the furrows, the man makes a snatch (잡아챔) in the air with his hands. He thinks I'm somewhere in the air. That's because I'm sitting on his think-furrows, and he can't work out (알다) so quickly where I really am. At last he does.

He mutters and jabs (세게 찌르다) at me. Now then, Miss Maya, or whatever your name is, now then, you've got to have your wits about you (have[keep] one's wits about one 빈틈없이 머리를 쓰다; (어떤 일에도) 당황[흥분]하지 않다). I see the hand coming, but I wait until the last moment, then I fly nimbly (재빠르게) to one side, sit down, and watch him feel to see if I am still there.—We kept the game up often for a full half hour. You have no idea what a lot of **endurance** (인내, 참을성) the man has. Finally he jumps up and pours (퍼붓다) out a string (일련, 줄, 무리) of words which show how ungrateful (불쾌한) he is. Well, what of it (그것을 어떻게 하겠어요)? A noble (고귀한) soul seeks (구하다) no reward (보답, 보상). I'm already up on the ceiling listening to his ungrateful (은혜를 모르는) outburst (감정 등의 폭발)."

"I can't say I particularly like it," observed Maya. "Isn't it rather useless (쓸모없는)?"

"Do you expect me to erect (세우다, 짓다) a honeycomb (벌집) on his nose?" exclaimed Puck. "You have no sense of humor, dear girl. What do you do that's useful (너는 무슨 쓸모있는 것을 하는데요)?"

Little Maya went red all over, but quickly **collect**ed (자제심을 되찾다, 모으다) herself to hide (숨기다) her embarrassment (당황) from Puck.

"The time is coming," she flashed (발끈하여 말하다, 확 불타다), "when I shall do something big and splendid, and good and useful too. But first I want to see what is going on in the world. Deep down in my heart I feel that the time is coming."

As Maya spoke she felt a hot **tide** (조류, 밀물) of hope and

enthusiasm (열정) flood (밀려오다, 홍수 나다) her being.

Puck seemed not to realize how serious (진지한) she was, and how deeply **stir**red (감동시키다, 선동하다). He zigzagged about in his **flurried** (혼란스러운) way for a while, then asked:

"You don't happen to have any honey with you, do you, my dear?"

"I'm so sorry," replied Maya. "I'd gladly let you have some, especially after you've entertained (즐겁게 하다) me so pleasantly, but I really haven't got any with me.—May I ask you one more question?"

"Shoot (쏘다, 즉시 하다)," said Puck. "I'll answer, I'll always answer."

"I'd like to know how I could get into a human being's house."

"Fly in," said Puck sagaciously (똑똑한 척(sagacious 현명한, 기민한)).

"But how, without running into (~와 만나다(into)) danger?"

"Wait until a window is opened. But be sure to find the way out again. Once you're inside, if you can't find the window, the best thing to do is to fly toward the light. You'll always find plenty of windows in every house. You need only notice where the sun shines through. Are you going already?"

"Yes," replied Maya, holding out (내밀다) her hand. "I have

some things to attend(돌보다) to. Good-by. I hope you quite recover(회복하다) from the effects(효과) of the ice age."

And with her fine confident(대담한, 자신 있는) buzz that yet sounded slightly anxious, little Maya raised her gleaming wings and flew out into the sunshine across to the flowery meadows(초원) to **cull**(꽃을 따 모으다, 추려 내다) a little **nourishment**(음식물, 영양).

Puck looked after her, and carefully **meditate**(곰곰이 생각하다, 명상하다)d what might still be said. Then he observed thoughtfully:

"Well, now. Well, well.—Why not?"

CHAPTER **07**

IN THE TOILS

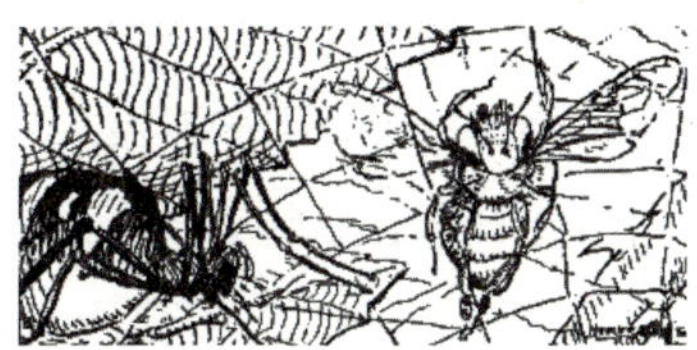

After her meeting with Puck the fly Maya was not in a particularly happy frame (마음의 상태, 틀) of mind. She could not bring herself to believe that he was right in everything he had said about human beings, or right in his relations (관계) to them. She had formed an entirely different **conception** (개념, 생각)—a much finer (더 좋은), lovelier picture, and she fought (fight (싸우다)의 과거) against letting her mind **harbor** (마음속에 품다, 숨겨주다, 항구) low or ridiculous (웃기는) ideas of mankind (인류). Yet she was still afraid to enter a human dwelling. How was she to know whether or not the owner (주인) would like it? And she wouldn't for all the world (절대로, 결코) make herself a burden (짐, 부담) to anyone.

Her thoughts went back once more to the things

Cassandra had told her.

"They are good and wise," Cassandra had said. "They are strong and powerful, but they never **abuse**(남용하다) their power. On the contrary, wherever they go they bring order(질서) and **prosperity**(번영). We bees, knowing they are friendly to us, put ourselves under their protection(보호) and share(나누다) our honey with them. They leave us enough for the winter, they provide(주다, 제공하다) us with shelter(피난처) against the cold, and guard us against the **host**s(다수, 많은 무리) of our enemies among the animals. There are few creatures in the world who have entered into such a relation of friendship and **voluntary**(자발적인) service with human beings. Among the insects you will often hear voices raised(크게 외치다, 올리다) to speak evil of(~을 나쁘게 말하다) man. Don't listen to them. If a foolish tribe(종족) of bees ever returns to the wild and tries to do without human beings, it soon **perish**es(멸망하다). There are too many beasts that **hanker**(갈망하다) for our honey, and often a whole bee-city—all its buildings, all its inhabitants(거주자)—has been ruthlessly(무자비하게) destroyed(파괴하다), merely(단지) because a senseless(무분별한) animal wanted to satisfy(만족시키다) its greed(탐욕) for honey."

That is what Cassandra had told Maya about human beings, and until Maya had convinced(납득시키다, 확신시키다) herself of the contrary(정반대), she wanted to keep this belief in them.

It was now afternoon. The sun was dropping behind the fruit trees in a large vegetable(야채) garden through which Maya was flying. The trees were long past flowering, but the little bee still remembered them in the shining glory of countless(수없이 많은) blossoms, whiter than light, lovely, pure, and exquisite(아름다운) against the blue of the heavens. The delicious perfume(향기, 향수), the gleam and the shimmer(어른거리는 빛)—oh, she'd never forget the **rapture**(기쁨, 환희) of it as long as she lived.

As she flew she thought of how all that beauty would come again, and her heart **expand**(팽창하다)ed with delight in the glory of the great world in which she was permitted(허락하다) to live.

At the end of the garden shone the starry(별 같은) tufts(다발, 장식 술) of the jasmine—delicate yellow faces set in a **wreath**(화환) of pure white—sweet perfume wafted(떠돌게 하다) to Maya on the soft wings of the breeze.

And weren't there still some trees in bloom(꽃)? Wasn't it the season(제철, 한창 때) for lindens(보리수)? Maya thought delightedly of the big serious lindens, whose tops held the red glow of the setting sun to the very last.

She flew in among the stems of the blackberry vines(덩굴), which were putting forth green berries and yielding(농작물 등을 생산하다, 내다) blossoms at the same time. As she mounted(오르다) again to reach the jasmine, something strange to the touch suddenly laid itself across her forehead and shoulders, and just as quickly covered her wings. It was the queerest(기묘한) sensation(느낌, 기분), as if her wings were **crippled**(부자유스럽게 하다, 불구를 만들다) and she were suddenly **restrain**ed(제한하다) in her flight, and were falling, helplessly(무력하게) falling. A secret(은밀한), wicked force(힘) seemed to be holding her feelers, her legs, her wings in invisible(보이지 않는) captivity(감금). But she did not fall. Though she could no longer move her wings, she still hung in the air rocking(흔들리는), caught by a marvelously yielding(잘 구부러지는, 유연한) softness(부드러움) and delicacy(섬세함), raised(올리다) a little, lowered(내리다) a little, tossed(가볍게 던지다) here, tossed there, like a loose(떨어진, 풀린) leaf in a faint(약한) breeze.

Maya was troubled, but not as yet actually terrified(겁먹은). Why should she be? There was no pain nor real discomfort(불편함) of any sort. Simply that it was so peculiar, so very peculiar, and something bad seemed to be **lurk**ing(잠복하다, 숨어 기다리고 있다) in the background(배후, 배경). She must get on(일을 계속 진행하다(빠져 나오는 일을)). If she tried very hard, she could, assuredly(확실히).

But now she saw a thread(실) across her breast, an elastic(탄력 있는) silvery thread finer than the finest silk. She clutched at it quickly, in a cold wave of terror. It clung to(~에 붙었다) her hand; it wouldn't shake off(흔들어 떼다). And there ran another silver thread over her shoulders. It drew itself across her wings and tied them together—her wings were powerless. And there, and there! Everywhere in the air and above her body—those bright, glittering, gluey(끈적끈적한) threads!

Maya screamed with horror. Now she knew! Oh—oh, now she knew! She was in a spider's web(거미줄).

Her terrified shrieks(비명) rang out(울렸다) in the silent dome(둥근 천장) of the summer day, where the sunshine touched(색조를 띠게 하다) the green of the leaves into gold, and insects flitted(휙 날다) to and fro, and birds **swoop**(급강하하다)ed gaily(유쾌하게) from tree to tree. Nearby, the jasmine sent its perfume into the air—the jasmine she had wanted to reach. Now all was over.

A small bluish(푸른 빛을 띤) butterfly, with brown dots(점) gleaming like copper(구릿빛, 구리) on its wings, came flying very close.

"Oh, you poor soul," it cried, hearing Maya's screams and seeing her desperate **plight**(곤경, 궁지). "May your death(죽음) be an easy one, lovely child. I cannot help you. Some day, perhaps this very night, I shall meet with the same fate. But meanwhile life is still lovely for me. Good-by. Don't forget the sunshine in the deep sleep of death."

And the blue butterfly rocked away, drugged((약에)취해; drug 약을 먹이다, 약) by the sunshine and the flowers and its own joy of living.

The tears streamed (흐르다) from Maya's eyes; she lost her last **shred** (조각, 단편) of self-control. She tossed her captive (붙들린) body to and fro, and buzzed (윙윙 대다(날개로)) as loud as she could, and screamed for help—from whom she did not know. But the more she tossed the tighter she **enmeshed** (말려들다, 그물에 걸리다) herself in the web. Now, in her great **agony** (괴로움, 고통), Cassandra's warnings (경고) went through her mind:

"Beware (조심하다) of the spider and its web. If we bees fall into the spider's power we suffer the most gruesome (소름끼치는) death. The spider is heartless and tricky (교활한), and once it has a person in its toils (올가미, 노고), it never lets him go."

In a great **flare** (타오름, 감정 등의 격발) of **mortal** (지독한, 죽을 운명의) terror Maya made one huge desperate (필사적인) effort. Somewhere one of the long, heavier **suspension** (매달기, 공중에 떠 있기) threads snapped (딱 부러지다). Maya felt it break, yet at the same time she sensed the awful **doom** (운명, 비운, 파멸) of the cobweb. This was, that the more one struggled (버둥거리다) in it, the more effectively and dangerously it worked. She gave up (포기했다), in complete exhaustion (지침).

At that moment she saw the spider herself—very near, under a blackberry leaf. At sight of the great monster, silent and serious, crouching (몸을 구부리다) there as if ready to pounce (갑자기 덤벼들다), Maya's horror was **indescribable** (말로 표현할 수 없는). The wicked shining eyes were fastened (고정시키다) on the little bee in sinister (사악한),

cold-blooded(냉혹한, 냉혈의) patience.

Maya gave one loud shriek. This was the worst agony of all. Death itself could look no worse than that grey, hairy monster with her mean fangs(엄니) and the raised legs supporting her fat body like a scaffolding(건축 등의 비계(발판)). She would come rushing upon her, and then all would be over.

Now a dreadful fury(분노) of anger came upon Maya, such as she had never felt before. Forgetting her great agony, intent(집중한) only upon one thing—selling her life as dearly as possible—she uttered her clear, alarming battle(전투)-cry, which all beasts knew and dreaded(두려워하다).

"You will pay for your cunning(교활함) with death," she shouted at the spider. "Just come and try to kill me, you'll find out what a bee can do."

The spider did not budge(움직이다). She really was **uncanny**(으스스한, 기괴한, 불가사의한) and must have terrified bigger creatures than little Maya.

Strong in her anger, Maya now made another violent, desperate effort. Snap! One of the long suspension threads above her broke. The web was probably meant for flies and gnats(각다귀), not for such large insects as bees.

But Maya got herself only more **entangle**d(얽히게 하다).

In one gliding motion the spider drew quite close

to Maya. She swung by her nimble legs upon a single thread with her body hanging (매달려 있다) straight downward.

"What right (권리) have you to break my net?" she rasped (귀에 거슬리는 소리로 말하다, 줄을 갈다) at Maya. "What are you doing here? Isn't the world big enough for you? Why do you disturb (방해하다) a peaceful **recluse** (은둔자)?"

That was not what Maya had expected to hear. Most certainly not.

"I didn't mean to," she cried, quivering (떨다) with glad hope. Ugly as the spider was, still she did not seem to intend (~하려 하다) any harm. "I didn't see your web and I got **tangle**d (엉키게 하다) in it. I'm so sorry. Please pardon me."

The spider drew nearer.

"You're a funny little body," she said, letting go of (~에서 떼다) the thread first with one leg, then with the other. The delicate thread shook. How wonderful that it could support (지탱하다, 지지하다) the great creature.

"Oh, do help me out of this," begged Maya, "I should be so grateful."

"That's what I came here for," said the spider, and smiled strangely. For all her smiling she looked mean (야비한) and deceitful (속이는). "Your tossing and tugging (세게 잡아당기는 것) spoils (망치다) the whole web. Keep quiet one second, and I will set you free."

"Oh, thanks! Ever so many thanks!" cried Maya.

The spider was now right beside her. She examined the web carefully to see how securely (단단히, 확고하게, 안전하게) Maya was entangled.

"How about your sting?" she asked.

Ugh, how mean and horrid (지독한) she looked! Maya fairly shivered with disgust at the thought that she was going to touch her, but replied as pleasantly as she could:

"Don't trouble about my sting. I will draw (끌어당기다) it in, and nobody can hurt himself on it then."

"I should hope not," said the spider. "Now, then, look out! Keep quiet. Too bad for my web."

Maya remained still. Suddenly she felt herself being whirled (빙빙 돌다) round and round on the same spot (장소), till she got dizzy (어지러운) and sick (구역질이 나는) and had to close her eyes.—But what was that? She opened her eyes quickly. Horrors! She was completely enmeshed (그물에 걸다) in a fresh sticky (끈적끈적한) thread which the spider must have had with her.

"My God!" cried little Maya softly, in a quivering voice. That was all she said. Now she saw how tricky the spider had been; now she was really caught beyond release(해방, 구출); now there was absolutely no chance of escape. She could no longer move any part of her body. The end was near.

Her fury of anger was gone, there was only a great sadness in her heart.

"I didn't know there was such meanness and wickedness in the world," she thought. "The deep night of death is upon me. Good-by, dear bright sun. Good-by, my dear friend-bees. Why did I leave you? A happy life to you. I must die."

The spider sat wary(경계하는, 조심하는), a little to one side. She was still afraid of Maya's sting.

"Well?" she jeered(조롱하다). "How are you feeling, little girl?"

Maya was too proud to answer the false(거짓말하는, 옳지 않은) creature. She merely said, after a while when she felt she couldn't bear any more:

"Please kill me right away."

"Really!" said the spider, tying a few torn(찢어진) threads together. "Really! Do you take(간주하다) me to be as big a dunce(바보) as yourself? You're going to die anyhow, if you're kept hanging long enough, and that's the time for me to suck(빨다) the blood out of you—when you can't sting. Too bad, though, that you can't see how dreadfully you've **damage**d my lovely web. Then you'd realize that you deserve to die."

She dropped down to the ground, laid the end of the newly spun thread about a stone, and pulled it in tight. Then she ran up again, caught hold of the thread by which little enmeshed Maya hung, and dragged her captive along.

"You're going into the shade, my dear," she said, "so that you shall not dry up out here in the sunshine. Besides, hanging here you're like a scarecrow, you'll frighten away other nice little mortals who don't watch where they're going. And sometimes the sparrows come and rob my web.—To let you know with whom you're dealing, my name is Thekla, of the family of cross-spiders. You needn't tell me your name. It makes no difference. You're a fat bit, and you'll taste just as tender and juicy by any name."

So little Maya hung in the shade of the blackberry vine, close to the ground, completely at the mercy of the cruel spider, who intended her to die by slow starvation. Hanging with her little head downward—a fearful position to be in—she soon felt she would not last many more minutes. She whimpered (흐느껴 울다) softly, and her cries for help grew feebler (더 약한, 더 희미한) and **feebler** (약한, 희미한). Who was there to hear? Her folk (가족) at home knew nothing of this **catastrophe** (재앙), so they couldn't come hurrying to her rescue (구조, 구출).

Suddenly down, in the grass, she heard some one growling:

"Make way! I'm coming."

Maya's agonized (괴로운) heart began to beat stormily (사납게, 난폭하게). She recognized the voice of Bobbie, the dung-beetle.

"Bobbie," she called, as loud as she could, "Bobbie, dear Bobbie!"

"Make way! I'm coming."

"But I'm not in your way, Bobbie," cried Maya. "Oh dear, I'm hanging over your head. The spider has caught me."

"Who are you?" asked Bobbie. "So many people know me. You know they do (know를 대신하는 대동사), don't you?"

"I am Maya—Maya, the bee. Oh please, please help me!"

"Maya? Maya?—Ah, now I remember. You made my acquaintance several weeks ago.—The 100 deuce (불행, 재난)! You are in a bad way, if I must say so myself. You certainly do need my help. As I happen to (우연히 ~하다) have a few moments' time, I won't refuse(거절하다)."

"Oh, Bobbie, can you tear these threads?"

"Tear those threads! Do you mean to insult me?" Bobbie slapped(찰싹 하고 소리를 내다) the muscles(근육) of his arm. "Look, little girl. Hard as steel(강철). No match(상대) for that in strength. I can do more than smash(박살내다) a few cobwebs. You'll see something that'll make you open your eyes."

Bobbie crawled up on the leaf, caught hold of the thread by which Maya was hanging, clung to it, then let go of the leaf. The thread broke, and they both fell to the ground.

"That's only the beginning," said Bobbie.—"But Maya, you're trembling. My dear child, you poor little girl, how pale you are! Now who would be so afraid of death? You must look death calmly in the face as I do. So. I'll unwrap(감은 것을 풀다) you now."

Maya could not utter a syllable(한마디(말의), 음절). Bright tears(눈물) of joy ran down her cheeks. She was to be free again, fly again in the sunshine, wherever she wished. She was to live.

But then she saw the spider coming down the blackberry vine.

"Bobbie," she screamed, "the spider's coming."

Bobbie went on unperturbed(침착한, 냉정한), merely laughing to himself. He really was an extraordinarily(몹시) strong insect.

"She'll think twice(두 번 생각하다(다시 생각하다)) before she comes nearer," he said.

But there! The **vile**(몹시 싫은, 비열한) voice rasped(귀에 거슬리는 소리로 말하다) above them:

"Robbers(강도)! Help! I'm being robbed(강도 당하다). You fat lump(덩어리, 땅딸보), what are you doing with my prey(먹이감)?"

"Don't excite yourself, madam," said Bobbie. "I have a right, haven't I, to talk to my friend. If you say another word to displease(불쾌하게 하다) me, I'll tear your whole web to shreds(조각). Well? Why so silent all of a sudden(갑자기)?"

"I am defeated(격퇴 당한, 진(defeat 격퇴하다, 이기다))," said the spider.

"That has nothing to do with the case(경우)," observed Bobbie. "Now you'd better be getting away from here."

The spider cast(던지다) a look at Bobbie full of hate and **venom**(악의, 원한, 독); but glancing up at her web she reconsidered(다시 생각하다), and turned away slowly, furious(화가 나), scolding and growling under her breath(작은 소리로). Fangs and stings were **of no avail**(소용 없는(avail 효용, 소용)). They wouldn't even leave a mark(표지) on armor(갑옷) such as Bobbie wore(입었다). With violent **denunciation**s(비난, 탄핵) against the injustice(부당함, 불법) in the world, the spider hid herself away inside a withered(시든) leaf, from which she could spy(몰래 감시하다) out and watch over her web.

Meanwhile Bobbie finished the unwrapping of Maya. He tore the network(그물) and released(풀어주다) her legs and wings. The rest she could do herself. She **preen**ed(몸치장을 하다) herself happily. But she had to go slow, because she was still weak from fright(공포, 경악).

"You must forget what you have been through," said Bobbie. "Then you'll stop trembling. Now see if you can fly. Try."

Maya lifted(들어올리다) herself with a little buzz. Her wings worked splendidly, and to her intense(강렬한) joy she felt that no part of her body had been injured(부상당하다). She flew slowly up to the jasmine flowers, drank **avidly**(열광적으로) of their abundant(풍부한) scented(향기로운) honey-juice, and returned to Bobbie, who had left the blackberry vines and was sitting in the grass.

"I thank you with my whole heart and soul," said Maya, deeply moved(감동 받은) and happy in her regained(다시 얻은) freedom(자유).

"Thanks are in place(적절한)," observed Bobbie. "But that's the way I always am—always doing something for other people. Now fly away. I'd advise(충고하다) you to lay your head on your pillow(베개) early to-night. Have you far to go?"

"No," said Maya. "Only a short way. I live at the edge of the beech (너도밤나무)-woods. Good-by, Bobbie, I'll never forget you, never, never, so long as (~하는 한) I live. Good-by."

CHAPTER 08

THE BUG AND THE BUTTERFLY

Her adventure with the spider gave Maya something to think about. She made up her mind to be more cautious in the future, not to rush(돌진하다) into things so recklessly(무모하게). Cassandra's **prudent**(분별 있는) warnings about the greatest dangers that threaten(위협하다) the bees, were enough to give one pause; and there were all sorts of other possibilities, and the world was such a big place—oh, there was a good deal to make a little bee stop and think.

It was in the evening particularly(특히), when twilight(황혼) fell and the little bee was all by herself, that one consideration(깊은 생각, 고려) after another stirred(부추기다, 강하게 움직이다) her mind. But the next morning, if the sun shone, she usually forgot half the things that had bothered her the night before, and allowed her eagerness (열망) for experiences to drive her out again into the gay whirl (소용돌이, 사건 등의 어지러운 연속) of life.

One day she met a very curious (이상한) creature. It was **angular** (모난, 각진) and flat as a pancake, but had a rather neat design (무늬) on its sheath (덮개); and whether its sheath were wings or what, you couldn't really tell. The odd little monster sat absolutely still (가만히) on the shaded leaf of a raspberry bush, its eyes half closed, apparently sunk (빠진, 가라앉은) in meditation (명상). The scent of the raspberries spread around it deliciously (향기롭게). Maya wanted to find out what sort of an animal it was. She flew to the next-door leaf and said how-do-you-do. The stranger made no reply.

"How do you do, again?" And Maya gave its leaf a little tap (가볍게 두드림). The flat object (물체) peeled (벗기다) one eye open, turned it on Maya, and said:

"A bee. The world is full of bees," and closed its eye again.

"**Unique** (독특한)," thought Maya, and determined (결심하다) to get at (확인하다, 알다, 닿다) the stranger's secret. For now it excited (자극하다) her curiosity (호기심) more than ever, as people often do who pay no attention (관심) to us. She tried honey. "I have plenty of honey," she said. "May I offer (주다) you some?" The stranger opened its one eye and regarded (응시하다) Maya contemplatively (명상하는 듯이) a moment or two. "What is it going to say this time?" Maya wondered.

This time there was no answer at all. The one eye merely closed again, and the stranger sat quite still, tight on the leaf, so that you couldn't see its legs and you'd have thought it had been pressed down flat with a thumb.

Maya realized, of course, that the stranger wanted to ignore (무시하다) her, but—you know how it is—you don't like being **snub**bed (냉대하다, 퇴짜 놓다), especially if you haven't found out what you wanted to find out. It makes you feel so cheap (보잘것없는, 하찮은, 값싼).

"Whoever you are," cried Maya, "permit me to inform (알리다) you that insects are in the habit (풍습, 습관) of greeting each other, especially when one of them happens to be a bee." The bug (벌레) sat on without budging (budge 움직이다). It did not so much as (~조차도 않다) open its one eye again. "It's ill (아픈)," thought Maya. "How horrid to be ill on a lovely day like this. That's why it's staying in the shade, too." She flew over to the bug's leaf and sat down beside it. "Aren't you feeling well?" she asked, so very friendly.

At this the funny creature began to move away. "Move" is the only word to use, because it didn't walk, or run, or fly, or hop. It went as if shoved(밀다) by an invisible hand.

"It hasn't any legs. That's why it's so cross(시무룩한, 언짢은)," thought Maya.

When it reached the stem of the leaf it stopped a second(초), moved on again, and, to her astonishment(놀라움), Maya saw that it had left behind a little brown drop(방울).

"How very **singular**(기묘한, 보기 드문)," she thought—and clapped(갖다 대다) her hand to her nose and held it tight shut(닫은). The veriest(very (대단히, 몹시)의 최상급) **stench**(악취) came from the little brown drop. Maya almost fainted(기절하다). She flew away as fast as she could and seated herself on a raspberry, where she held on to her nose and shivered with disgust and excitement(흥분).

"Serves you right(그런 대접을 받을 만하다, 당연하다)," someone above her called, and laughed. "Why take up with(사귀다, 친해지다) a stink-bug(노린재(stink 악취가 나다))?"

"Don't laugh!" cried Maya.

She looked up. A white butterfly had alighted(내리다) overhead on a slender(가느다란), swaying(흔들리는) branch of the raspberry bush, and was slowly opening and closing its broad wings—slowly, softly, silently, happy in the sunshine—black corners to its wings, round black marks in the centre of each wing, four round black marks in all. Ah, how beautiful, how beautiful! Maya forgot her **vexation**(화남, 신경질). And she was glad, too, to talk to the butterfly. She had never made the acquaintance of one before even though she had met a great many.

"Oh," she said, "you probably are right to laugh. Was that a stink-bug?"

"It was," he replied, still smiling. "The sort of person to keep away from (~로부터 떨어지다, 사귀지 않다). You're probably very young still?"

"Well," observed Maya, "I shouldn't say I was—exactly. I've been through a great deal. But that was the first specimen (실례, 견본) of the kind I had ever come across. Can you imagine doing such a thing ((왜)그러한 것을(노린재가) 하는지 상상할 수 있어요)?"

The butterfly had to laugh again.

"You see," he explained, "stink-bugs like to keep to themselves (그들 혼자 있다). They are not very popular (인기 있는), so they use the **odoriferous** (악취를 풍기는, 향기 나는) drop to make people take notice of (~을 알아차리다) them. We'd probably soon forget the fact of their existence (존재) if it were not for the drop: it serves as a reminder (생각나게 하는 것). And they want to be remembered (기억하다), no matter how (어떻게 해서든)."

"How lovely, how exquisitely lovely your wings are," said Maya. "So delicate (섬세한) and white. May I introduce myself? Maya, of the nation of bees."

The butterfly laid his wings together to look like only one wing standing straight up in the air. He gave a slight bow(인사).

"Fred," he said **laconically**((말을) 간결하게).

Maya couldn't gaze(응시하다) her fill(가득함).
(그녀가 충분하도록 볼 수 없었다-나비가 너무 예뻐 보고 또 보아도 질리지 않는다)

"Fly a little," she asked.

"Shall I fly away?"

"Oh no. I just want to see your great white wings move in the blue air. But never mind. I can wait till later. Where do you live?"

"Nowhere specially. A settled(정해진) home is too much of a **nuisance**(귀찮은 존재). Life didn't get to be really delightful until I turned into a butterfly. Before that, while I was still a caterpillar(애벌레), I couldn't leave the cabbage(양배추) the livelong(시간이 긴) day, and all one did was eat and **squabble**(쓸데없는 싸움을 하다)."

"Just what do you mean?" asked Maya, mystified(어리둥절해).

"I used to(과거에 ~였다(현재는 아님)) be a caterpillar," explained Fred.

"Never!" cried Maya.

"Now, now, now," said Fred, pointing(가리키다) both feelers straight at Maya. "Everyone knows a butterfly is first a caterpillar. Even human beings know it."

Maya was utterly(철저히, 완전히) perplexed(당혹한). Could such a thing(그런 일이 있을 수 있을까)

be?

"You must really explain more clearly," she said. "I couldn't accept what you say just so, could I? You wouldn't expect (기대하다) me to."

The butterfly perched beside the little bee on the slender swaying branch of the raspberry bush, and they rocked (흔들리다) together in the morning wind. He told her how he had begun life as a caterpillar and then, one day, when he had **shed** (벗기다) his last caterpillar skin, he came out (~이 되었다) a **pupa** (번데기) or **chrysalis** (고치, 번데기).

"At the end of a few weeks," he continued, "I woke up out of my dark sleep and broke through the wrappings (포장) or pupa-case (그릇, 통). I can't tell you, Maya, what a feeling comes over (느낌이 들다, 덮치다) you when, after a time like that, you suddenly see the sun again. I felt as though I were melting (녹다) in a warm golden ocean, and I loved my life so that my heart began to pound (쿵쾅거리다)."

"I understand," said Maya, "I understand. I felt the same way the first time I left our **humdrum** (단조로운, 지루한) city and flew out into the bright scented world of blossoms." The little bee was silent a while, thinking of her first flight.— But then she wanted to know how the butterfly's large wings could grow in the small space of the pupa-case.

Fred explained.

"The wings are delicately folded(접힌) together like the petals(꽃잎) of a flower in the bud(꽃봉오리). When the weather is bright and warm, the flower must open, it cannot help itself, and its petals unfold(펼치다, 접힌 것을 펴다). So with my wings, they were folded up, then unfolded. No one can resist(저항하다) the sun when it shines(비추다)."

"No, no—one cannot—one cannot resist the sunshine." Maya mused(생각에 잠기다), watching the butterfly as he perched in the golden light of the morning, pure white against the blue sky.

"People often charge(비난하다, 책망하다) us with being **frivolous**(경망스러운)," said Fred. "We're really happy—just that—just happy. You wouldn't believe how seriously I sometimes think about life."

"Tell me what all you think."

"Oh," said Fred, "I think about the future. It's very interesting to think about the future.—But I should like to fly now. The meadows on the hillside(산허리) are full of yarrow(서양가세풀) and canterbury bells; everything's in bloom. I'd like to be there, you know."

This Maya understood, she understood it well, and they said good-by and flew away in different directions(방향),

the white butterfly rocking silently as if wafted (가볍게 보내다, 떠돌다) by the gentle wind, little Maya with that uneasy (안정되지 않은) zoom (붕하는 소리)-zoom of the bees which we hear upon the flowers on fair (날씨가 좋은) days and which we always recall (상기하다) when we think of the summer.

CHAPTER **09**

THE LOST LEG

Near the hole where Maya had set herself up for the summer lived a family of bark(나무 껍질)-boring(bore 구멍을 뚫다) beetles. Fridolin, the father, was an earnest(성실한), industrious(부지런한) man who wanted many children and took immense(엄청난, 거대한) pains(수고, 고통) to bring up(키우다) a large family. He had done very well: he had fifty energetic(정력적인) sons to fill him with pride and high hopes. Each had dug(팠다) his own **meandering**(굽이도는, 구불구불한) little tunnel in the bark of the pine-tree and all were getting on and were comfortably settled.

"My wife," Fridolin said to Maya, after they had known each other some time, "has arranged(배열하다) things so that none of my sons **interfere**(방해하다, 간섭하다)s with the others. They are not even acquainted (알고 있는, 사귀게 된); each goes his own way."

Maya knew that human beings were none too fond of Fridolin and his people, though she herself liked him and liked his opinions (의견) and had found no reason to avoid (피하다) him. In the morning before the sun arose and the woods were still asleep, she would hear his fine tapping and boring (구멍 뚫는 것). It sounded like a delicate trickling (똑똑 떨어지는 것; trickle 조금씩 흐르다), or as if the tree were breathing in its sleep. Later she would see the thin brown dust (가루, 먼지) that he had emptied (비워졌다) out of his **corridor** (복도(나무에 판 구멍을 말함)).

Once he came at an early hour, as he often did, to wish her good-morning and ask if she had slept well.

"Not flying to-day?" he inquired.

"No, it's too windy."

It was windy. The wind rushed and roared (굉음을 내다) and flung the branches into a mad **tumult** (떠들썩함, 폭동). The leaves looked ready to fly away. After each great gust (돌풍) the sky would brighten (밝아지다), and in the pale light the trees seemed balder (더 잎이 없는(나무가); bald 대머리의, 잎이 없는). The pine in which Maya and Fridolin lived shrieked with the voices of the wind as in a fury (격분, 격노) of anger and excitement.

Fridolin sighed.

"I worked all night," he told Maya, "all night. But what can you do? You've got to do something to get somewhere. And I'm not altogether satisfied [만족한] with this pine; I should have **tackle**d [착수하다] a fir [전나무]-tree." He wiped his brow and smiled in self-pity [자기 연민].

"How are your children?" asked Maya pleasantly.

"Thank you," said Fridolin, "thank you for your interest. But"—he hesitated—"but I don't supervise [감독하다] the way I used to. Still, I have reason to believe they are all doing well."

As he sat there, a little brown man with slightly **curtail**ed [줄이다, 단축하다] wing-sheaths and a breastplate [가슴받이] that looked like a head too large for its body, Maya thought he was almost comical [웃기게 생긴, 웃긴]; but she knew he was a dangerous beetle who could do immense harm [해] to the mighty [거대한] trees of the forest, and if his tribe attacked [공격하다] a tree in numbers [떼 지어] then the green needles [바늘(녹색의 바늘들–침엽수(소나무나 전나무 같은)] were doomed [죽다], the tree would turn **sear** [시든, 마른, 태워 그을리다] and die. It was utterly without defenses [방어] against the little marauders [약탈자(maraud 약탈하려고 습격하다)] who destroyed the bark and the sap-wood [백목질(白木質) (나무의 껍질과 심 사이의 연한 부분/sap 수액)]. And the sap-wood is necessary [필수적인] to the life of a tree because it carries the sap up to the very tips [끝] of the branches. There were stories of how whole forests had fallen victims [희생자] to the race of boring-beetles. Maya looked at Fridolin reflectively [생각에 잠겨]; she was awed [두려움을 느끼게 하다] into **solemnity** [엄숙함] at the thought of the great power these little creatures

possessed (가지다) and of how important they could become.

Fridolin sighed and said in a worried tone:

"Ah, life would be beautiful if there were no woodpeckers (딱따구리)."

Maya nodded.

"Yes, indeed, you're right. The woodpecker gobbles (통째로 삼키다) up every insect he sees."

"If it were only that," observed Fridolin, "if it were only that he got the careless (부주의한) people (사람(곤충을 말함)) who fool around (빈둥거리다) on the outside, on the bark, I'd say, 'Very well, a woodpecker must live too.' But it seems all wrong that the bird should follow us right into our corridors into the remotest (가장 외딴, 가장 떨어진 / remote 외딴, 멀리 떨어진) corners of our homes."

"But he can't. He's too big, isn't he?"

Fridolin looked at Maya with an air of grave (진지한) importance (중요함), lifting his brows and shaking his head two or three times. It seemed to please him that he knew something she didn't know.

"Too big? What difference (차이) does his size make? No, my dear, it's not his size we are afraid of; it's his tongue."

Maya made big eyes.

Fridolin told her about the woodpecker's tongue:

that it was long and thin, and round as a worm, and **barbed**(가시가 있는) and sticky(끈적한).

"He can stretch(뻗다) his tongue out ten times my length," cried the bark-beetle, **flourish**ing(팔 등을 휘두르다) his arm. "You think: 'now—now he has reached the limit(한계), he can't make it the tiniest(tiny (작은)의 최상급) bit longer.' But no, he goes on stretching and stretching it. He pokes(찌르다) it deep into all the cracks(깨진 틈) and **crevice**s(갈라진 틈) of the bark, on the chance that he'll find somebody sitting there. He even pushes it into our passageways(통로)—actually, into our corridors and chambers. Things stick(붙다) to it, and that's the way he pulls us out of our homes."

"I am not a coward(겁쟁이)," said Maya, "I don't think I am, but what you say makes me creepy(섬뜩한)."

"Oh, you're all right," said Fridolin, a little envious(부러운 듯한), "you with your sting are safe. A person'll think twice before he'll let you sting his tongue. Anybody'll tell you that. But how about us bark-beetles? How do you think we feel? A cousin(사촌) of mine got caught. We had just had a little quarrel(다툼, 싸움) on account of(~때문에) my wife. I remember every detail(자세한 것) perfectly. My cousin was paying us a visit and hadn't yet got used to our ways or our arrangements(배열). All of a sudden we heard a woodpecker scratching(긁다) and boring—one of the smaller species. It must have begun right at our building because as a rule (일반적으로) we hear him beforehand (미리) and have time to run to shelter (대피소) before he reaches us.

"Suddenly I heard my poor cousin scream in the dark: 'Fridolin, I'm sticking!' Then all I heard was a short desperate scuffle (드잡이, 난투), followed by complete silence, and in a few moments the woodpecker was hammering (두들기다) at the house next door. My poor cousin! Her name was Agatha."

"Feel how my heart is beating," said Maya, in a whisper. "You oughtn't to have told it so quickly. My goodness, the things that do happen!" And the little bee thought of her own adventures in the past and the accidents that might still happen to her.

A laugh from Fridolin interrupted (중단시키다) her reflections (숙고, 생각). She looked up in surprise.

"See who's coming," he cried, "coming up the tree. Here's the fellow for you! I tell you, he's a—but you'll see."

Maya followed the direction of his gaze and saw a remarkable (진기한, 범상치 않은) animal slowly climbing up the trunk. She wouldn't have believed such a creature was possible if she had not seen it with her own eyes.

"Hadn't we better hide?" she asked, alarm getting the better of (get[gain, have] the better of ... 〈상대를〉 능가하다, 패배시키다) astonishment.

"Absurd (불합리한, 어리석은)," replied the bark-beetle, "just sit still and be polite (공손한) to the gentleman. He is very learned (학식 있는), really, very scholarly (학자다운), and what is more (더군다나), kind and modest (겸손한) and, like most persons of his type, rather funny. See what he's doing now!"

"Probably thinking," observed Maya, who couldn't get over (극복하다) her astonishment.

"He's struggling against the wind," said Fridolin, and laughed. "I hope his legs don't get entangled (엉킨)."

"Are those long threads really his legs?" asked Maya, opening her eyes wide. "I've never seen the like (종류)."

Meanwhile the newcomer (새로 온 사람) had drawn near, and Maya got a better view of him. He looked as though he were swinging (그네처럼 흔들리다) in the air, his rotund (동그란) little body hung so high on his monstrously (괴물 같이) long legs, which groped (더듬다) for a footing (발판) on all sides like a movable (움직일 수 있는) scaffolding (건축 등의 비계(발판)) of threads. He stepped (발걸음을 옮기다) along cautiously (조심스럽게), feeling (만지다, 느끼다) his way; the little brown sphere (구) of his body rose and sank (가라앉았다), rose and sank. His legs were so very long and thin that one alone would certainly (분명히) not have been enough (충분한) to support (지지하다)

his body. He needed all at once, unquestionably. As they were jointed in the middle, they rose high in the air above him.

Maya clapped her hands together.

"Well!" she cried. "Did you ever? Would you have dreamed that such delicate legs, legs as fine as a hair, could be so nimble and useful—that one could really use them—and they'd know what to do? Fridolin, I think it's wonderful, simply wonderful."

"Ah, bah," said the bark-beetle. "Don't take things so seriously. Just laugh when you see something funny; that's all."

"But I don't feel like laughing. Often we laugh at something and later find out it was just because we haven't understood."

By this time the stranger had joined them and was looking down at Maya from the height of his pointed triangles of legs.

"Good-morning," he said, "a real wind-storm—a pretty strong draught, don't you think, or—no? You are of a different opinion?" He clung to the tree as hard as he could.

Fridolin turned to hide his laughing, but little

Maya replied politely that she quite agreed with him and that was why she had not gone out flying. Then she introduced herself. The stranger squinted (눈을 가늘게 뜨고 보다) down at her through his legs.

"Maya, of the nation of bees," he repeated. "Delighted, really. I have heard a good deal about bees.—I myself belong to the general (일반적인) family of spiders, species daddy-long-legs (긴 다리를 가진 곤충), and my name is Hannibal."

The word spider has an evil sound in the ears of all smaller insects, and Maya could not quite conceal (숨기다) her fright, especially as she was reminded of her agony (고통) in Thekla's web. Hannibal seemed to take no notice, so Maya decided, "Well if need (필요하다) be I'll fly away, and he can whistle for (구하여도[바라도] 소용없다) me; he has no wings and his web is somewhere else."

"I am thinking," said Hannibal, "thinking very hard.—If you will permit me, I will come a little closer. That big branch there makes a good shield (방패) against the wind."

"Why, certainly," said Maya, making room for him.

Fridolin said good-by and left. Maya stayed; she was eager to get at Hannibal's **personality** (성격, 인격).

"The many, many different kinds of animals there are in the world," she thought. "Every day a fresh discovery (발견)."

The wind had subsided (가라앉다, 진정되다) some, and the sun shone through the branches. From below rose the song of a robin redbreast, filling the woods with joy. Maya could see it perched on a branch, could see its throat swell (부풀다) and pulse (맥박 치다) with the song as it held its little head raised up to the light.

"If only I could sing like that robin redbreast," she said, "I'd perch on a flower and keep it up (계속하다(노래를)) the livelong day."

"You'd produce (생산하다, 만들다) something lovely, you would, with your humming and buzzing."

"The bird looks so happy."

"You have great fancies (상상들)," said the daddy-long-legs. "Supposing (suppose 가정해보자) every animal were to wish he could do something that nature had not fitted (능력을 주다, 적합하게 하다) him to do, the world would be all topsy-turvy (엉망인, 뒤죽박죽인). Supposing a robin redbreast thought he had to have a sting—a sting above everything else (무엇보다도)—or a goat wanted to fly about gathering (모으다) honey. Supposing a frog were to come along and languish (낙담한, 기운이 없는) for my kind of legs."
(네 종류와 같은 다리를 원하지만 얻을 수 없어 낙담한)

Maya laughed.

"That isn't just what I mean. I mean, it seems lovely to be able to make all beings as happy as the bird does with his song.—But goodness gracious (에구머니나)!" she exclaimed suddenly. "Mr. Hannibal, you have one leg too many (one too many 하나만큼 더 많다[남다]; 도가 지나치다)."

Hannibal frowned (얼굴을 찌푸리다) and looked into space, vexed (초조한).

"Well, you've noticed it," he said glumly (침울하게). "But as a matter of fact (사실)—one leg too few (다리 하나가 적다), not too many."

"Why? Do you usually have eight legs?"

"Permit me to explain. We spiders have eight legs. We need them all. Besides, eight is a more **aristocratic** (귀족의) number. One of my legs got lost. Too bad about it. However you manage, you make the best of (가장 잘 이용하다) it."

"It must be dreadfully disagreeable (불쾌한) to lose a leg," Maya **sympathize**d (동정하다).

Hannibal propped (기대다) his chin on his hand and arranged (배열하다) his legs to keep them from being easily counted (세다).

"I'll tell you how it happened. Of course, as usual when there's mischief (위해, 재해), a human being is mixed up in (좋지 않은 일과 관련이 있다) it. We spiders are careful and look what we're doing, but human beings are careless (부주의한), they grab (붙잡다) you sometimes as though you were a piece of wood. Shall I tell you?"

"Oh, do please," said Maya, settling(settle정하다) herself comfortably. "It would be awfully interesting. You must certainly have gone through a good deal(많은 것을 경험했다)."

"I should say so," said Hannibal. "Now listen. We daddy-long-legs, you know, hunt by night. I was then living in a green garden-house. It was overgrown(지나치게 자란) with ivy(담쟁이덩굴), and there were a number of broken window-panes, which made it very convenient(편리한) for me to crawl in and out. The man came at dark. In one hand he carried his **artificial**(인공의) sun, which he calls lamp, in the other hand a small bottle, under his arm some paper, and in his pocket another bottle. He put everything down on the table and began to think, because he wanted to write his thoughts on the paper.—You must certainly have come across paper in the woods or in the garden. The black on the paper is what man has excogitated(생각해내다)—excogitated."

"Marvelous!" cried Maya, all a-glow(흥분, 빛) that she was to learn so much.

"For this purpose," Hannibal continued, "man needs both bottles. He **insert**(삽입하다)s a stick(막대기(펜대를 의미함)) into the one and drinks out of the other. The more he drinks, the better it goes. Of course it is about us insects that he writes, everything he knows about us, and he writes **strenuously**(정력적으로, 활발히),

but the result is not much to **boast** (자랑스럽게 말하다) of, because up to now man has found out very little in regard to (~에 관하여) insects. He is absolutely ignorant (모르는) of our soul-life and hasn't the least consideration (고려, 숙고) for our feelings. You'll see."

"Don't you think well of (좋게 생각하다) human beings?" asked Maya.

"Oh, yes, yes. But the loss of a leg"—the daddy-long-legs looked down slantwise (비스듬하게)—"is **apt** (~하기 쉬운) to **embitter** (적개심을 품게 하다) one, rather."

"I see," said Maya.

"One evening I was sitting on a window-frame (틀) as usual, prepared (준비하다) for the chase (사냥, 추적), and the man was sitting at the table, his two bottles before him, trying to produce something. It annoyed (화나게 하다) me dreadfully that a whole swarm (떼, 무리) of little flies and gnats, upon which I depend (의지하다(up(on))) for my **subsistence** (존재, 생존), had settled upon the artificial sun and were staring into it in that crude (조심성이 없는, 허술한), stupid, uneducated way of theirs."

"Well," observed Maya, "I think I'd look at a thing like that myself."

"Look, for all I care (조금도 상관없다). But to look and to stare like an idiot (바보) are two entirely different things. Just watch once and see the silly jig (지그 춤) they dance around a lamp. It's nothing for them to **butt** (머리로 받다) their heads about twenty times. Some of them keep it up until they burn (태우다) their wings. And all the time they stare and stare at the light."

"Poor creatures (동물, 생물)! Evidently they lose their wits (건전한 정신, 지성)."

"Then they had better (~하는 게 낫다) stay outside on the window-frame or under the leaves. They're safe from the lamp there, and that's where I can catch them.—Well, on that fateful (운명의) night I saw from my position on the window-frame that some gnats were lying scattered (흩어져 있는) on the table beside the lamp drawing ((숨 등을) 들이쉬다) their last breath. The man did not seem to notice or care about them, so I decided to go and take them myself. That's perfectly natural (자연스러운), isn't it?"

"Perfectly."

"And yet, it was my undoing (파멸). I crept up the leg of the table, very softly, on my guard ((내가) 경계하여), until I could peep (엿보다) over the edge. The man seemed dreadfully big. I watched him working. Then, slowly, very slowly, carefully lifting one leg at a time (한번에), I crossed over to the lamp. As long as I was covered by the bottle all went well, but I had scarcely (~하자 마자 when~ 하다) turned the corner, when the man looked up and grabbed (잡아채다) me. He lifted me by one of my legs, dangled (매달아 늘어뜨리다) me in front of his huge eyes, and said: 'See what's here, just see what's here.' And he grinned—the brute!—he grinned with his whole face, as though it were a laughing matter(웃긴 일)."

Hannibal sighed, and little Maya kept quite still. Her head was in a whirl(혼란, 소동).

"Have human beings such immense eyes?" she asked at last.

"Please think of me in the position I was in," cried Hannibal, vexed. "Try to imagine how I felt. Who'd like to be hanging by the leg in front of eyes twenty times as big as his own body and a mouth full of gleaming(번뜩이는) teeth, each fully twice as big as himself? Well, what do you think?"

"Awful! Perfectly awful!"

"Thank the Lord, my leg broke off. There's no telling(말할 필요가 없다) what might have happened if my leg had not broken off. I fell to the table, and then I ran, I ran as fast as my remaining(남아 있는) legs would take me, and hid behind the bottle. There I stood and **hurl**ed(퍼붓다(욕설 등을), 세게 던지다) threats(위협) of violence((말의) 격함, 폭력) at the man. They saved me, my threats did, the man was afraid to run after me. I saw him lay my leg on the white paper, and I watched how it wanted to escape—which it can't do without me."

"Was it still moving?" asked Maya, prickling(prickle 가볍게 찌르다) at the thought.

"Yes. Our legs always do move when they're pulled out (당겨 뽑히다). My leg ran, but I not being there it didn't know where to run to, so it merely flopped (퍼덕거리다, 쿵 쓰러지다) about aimlessly (목적 없이) on the same spot, and the man watched it, clutching (움켜잡다) at his nose and smiling—smiling, the heartless wretch (치사한 놈, 불운한 사람)!—at my leg's sense (의식) of duty (의무)." (의무를 하려는 내 다리를 보고 웃다)

"Impossible," said the little bee, quite scared, "an offen leg can't crawl."

"An offen leg? What is an offen leg?"

"A leg that has come off," explained Maya, staring at him. "Don't you know? At home we children used the word offen for anything that had come off (떨어지다)."

"You should drop your **nursery** (아이들 방, 육아실) slang (속어) when you're out in the world and in the presence (면전, 있음) of cultured (교양 있는) people," said Hannibal severely (엄하게). "But it is true that our legs totter (비트적거리다, 아장아장 걷다) long after they have been torn (tear (찢다)의 과거분사) from our bodies."

"I can't believe it without proof (증거)."

"Do you think I'll tear one of my legs off to satisfy (만족시키다) you?" Hannibal's tone was ugly (험악한). "I see you're not a fit (적합한) person to **associate** (사귀다, 제휴하다) with. Nobody, I'd like you to know, nobody has ever doubted my word before."

Maya was terribly put out (난처하게 되었다). She couldn't understand what had upset (마음을 뒤집어놓다) the daddy-long-legs so, or what dreadful thing she had done.

"It isn't altogether easy to get along with (~와 잘 지내다) strangers (낯선 사람)," she thought. "They don't think the way we do and don't see that we mean no harm." She was depressed (우울한) and cast a troubled (당혹한) look at the spider with his long legs and soured (불쾌한, sour 시게 하다) expression (표정).

"Really, someone ought to come and eat you up."

Hannibal had evidently mistaken (잘못 여겼다) Maya's good nature for weakness (약함). For now something unusual (드문, 유별난) happened to the little bee. Suddenly her depression (우울) passed and gave way (양보했다), not to alarm or **timidity** (소심함), but to a calm courage (대담함). She straightened (곧게 하다) up, lifted her lovely, transparent (투명한) wings, uttered her high clear buzz, and said with a gleam in her eyes:

"I am a bee, Mr. Hannibal."

"I beg your pardon," said he, and without saying good-by turned and ran down the tree-trunk as fast as a person can run who has seven legs.

Maya had to laugh, willy-nilly (싫든 좋든, 할 수 없이). From down below Hannibal began to scold.

"You're bad. You threaten helpless people, you threaten them with your sting when you know they're **handicapped** by a misfortune and can't get away fast. But your hour is coming, and when you're in a tight place you'll think of me and be sorry." Hannibal disappeared under the leaves of the coltsfoot on the ground. His last words had not reached the little bee.

The wind had almost died away, and the day promised to be fine. White clouds sailed aloft in a deep, deep blue, looking happy and serene like good thoughts of the Lord. Maya was cheered. She thought of the rich shaded meadows by the woods and of the sunny slopes beyond the lake. A **blithe** activity must have begun there by this time. In her mind she saw the slim grasses waving and the purple iris that grew in the rills at the edge of the woods. From the flower of an iris you could look across to the mysterious night of the pine-forest and catch its cool breath of melancholy. You knew that its forbidding silence, which transformed the sunshine into a reddish half-light of sleep, was the home of the fairy tale.

Maya was already flying. She had started off instinctively, in answer to the call of the meadows and their gay carpeting of flowers. It was a joy to be alive.

CHAPTER 10

THE WONDERS OF THE NIGHT

Thus the days and weeks of her young life passed for little Maya among the insects in a lovely summer world—a happy roving (rove 방랑하다) in garden and meadow, occasional (때때로의) risks and many joys. For all that, she often missed the companions (친구) of her early childhood and now and again suffered (괴로워하다) a **pang** (상심, 비통, 번민) of homesickness (향수병), an ache (아픔) of longing (동경) for her people and the kingdom she had left. There were hours, too, when she **yearn**ed (그리워하다) for regular (정기적인, 규칙적인), useful work and **association** (교제, 조합) with friends of her own kind.

However, at bottom she had a restless (가만히 있지 않는) nature, little Maya had, and was scarcely ready to settle down (정착하다) for good (영원히) and live in the community (지역 공동체) of the bees; she wouldn't have felt comfortable. Often among animals as well(~뿐만 아니라) as human beings there are some who cannot **conform**(규칙 등에 따르다) to the ways of the others. Before we condemn(비난하다) them we must be careful and give them a chance to prove themselves. For it is not always laziness(게으름) or stubbornness(완고함) that makes them different. Far from(전혀 아니다) it. At the back of their peculiar urge(충동, 추진력) is a deep longing for something higher or better than what every-day life has to offer, and many a time(자주, 여러 번) young runaways(가출인, 도망자) have grown up into good, sensible(현명한), experienced(경험 있는) men and women.

Little Maya was a pure, sensitive(섬세한) soul, and her attitude(태도, 몸가짐) to the big, beautiful world came of a **genuine**(진지한, 진짜의) eagerness for knowledge and a great delight in the glories of creation.

Yet it is hard to be alone even when you are happy, and the more Maya went through, the greater became her yearning(동경) for companionship(사귐, 교제) and love. She was no longer so very young; she had grown into a strong, superb(당당한, 훌륭한) creature with sound(건강한), bright wings, a sharp, dangerous sting, and a highly developed(발전한) sense of both the pleasures and the **hazard**(위험)s of her life. Through her own experience she had gathered information(정보) and stored up(저장하다) wisdom(지혜), which she now often wished she could **apply**(사용하다, 활용하다) to something of real value. There were days when she was ready to return to the hive and throw herself at the queen's feet and **sue** (청원하다, 고소하다) for pardon (사면, 용서) and honorable reinstatement (복위(꿀벌 사회의 일원으로), 복직). But a great, burning desire held her back (저지했다)—the desire to know human beings. She had heard so many **contradictory** (상반되는, 모순되는) things about them that she was confused (혼란한) rather than enlightened (잘 알고 있는, 개화된). Yet she had a feeling that in the whole of creation there were no beings more powerful or more intelligent or more **sublime** (숭고한, 장엄한) than they.

A few times in her wanderings (방랑, 정처 없는 여행) she had seen people, but only from afar, from high up in the air—big and little people, black people, white people, red people, and such as dressed in many colors. She had never ventured (모험적으로 ~하다) close. Once she had caught the glimmer of red near a brook, and thinking it was a bed of flowers had flown down. She found a human being fast asleep among the brookside (시냇가) blossoms. It had golden hair and a pink face and wore a red dress. It was dreadfully large, of course, but still it looked so good and sweet that Maya thrilled (흥분했다), and tears came to her eyes. She lost all sense of her whereabouts (위치, 소재); she could do nothing but gaze and gaze upon the slumbering (자는) presence (존재). All the horrid things she had ever heard against man seemed utterly impossible.

Lies they must have been—mean lies that she had been told against creatures as charming as this one asleep in the shade of the whispering birch-trees.

After a while a mosquito came and buzzed greetings.

"Look!" cried Maya, hot with excitement and delight. "Look, just look at that human being there. How good, how beautiful! Doesn't it fill you with enthusiasm?"

The mosquito gave Maya a surprised stare, then turned slowly round to glance at the object of her admiration.

"Yes, it is good. I just tasted it. I stung it. Look, my body is shining red with its blood."

Maya had to press her hand to her heart, so startled was she by the mosquito's daring.

"Will it die?" she cried. "Where did you wound it? How could you? How could you screw up your courage to sting it? And how vile! Why, you're a beast of prey!"

The mosquito tittered.

"Why, it's only a very little human being," it answered in its high, thin voice. "It's the size called girl—the size at which the legs are covered half way up with a **separate**(별도의, 개개의) colored casing(포장, 싸개(무릎까지 오는 색깔 있는 양말을 말함)). My sting, of course, goes through the casing but usually doesn't reach the skin.—Your ignorance is really stupendous(놀랄 만한). Do you actually think that human beings are good? I haven't come across one who willingly(자진해서) let me take the tiniest drop of his blood."

"I don't know very much about human beings, I admit," said Maya humbly(겸손히).

"But of all the insects you bees have most to do with human beings(인간과 가장 관련이 많다). That's a well-known fact."

"I left our kingdom," Maya confessed(고백하다) timidly. "I didn't like it. I wanted to learn about the outside world."

"Well, well, what do you think of that!" The mosquito drew a step nearer. "How do you like your free-lancing(freelance(무소속, 자유계약자), 프리랜서)? I must say, I admire you for your independence(독립). I for one would never consent(동의하다, 승낙하다) to serve human beings."

"But they serve us too!" said Maya, who couldn't bear(참다) a slight(무시, 얕봄) to be put upon her people.

"Maybe.—To what nation do you belong?"

"I come of the nation in the castle park. The ruling(지배하는) queen is Helen VIII."

"Indeed," said the mosquito, and bowed low. "An **enviable**(부러운, 샘나는) **lineage**(혈통, 가계). My deepest respects.—There was a revolution (혁명) in your kingdom not so long ago, wasn't there? I heard it from the messengers (전령) of the **rebel** (반항자, 반역자) swarm. Am I right?"

"Yes," said Maya, proud and happy that her nation was so respected and renowned (유명한). Homesickness for her people awoke again, deep down in her heart, and she wished she could do something good and great for her queen and country. Carried away (carry away 넋을 잃게 하다) on the wings of this dream, she forgot to ask about human beings. Or, **like as not** (아마, 십중팔구), she **refrain**(삼가다, 억제하다)ed from questions, feeling that the mosquito would not tell her things she would be glad to hear. The mite (아주 작은 것, 진드기) of a creature impressed (인상 지우다) her as a saucy (뻔뻔스러운) Miss, and people of her kind usually had nothing good to say of others. Besides, she soon flew away.

"I'm going to take one more drink," she called back to Maya. "Later I and my friends are going flying in the light of the westering (서쪽으로 가는 (wester 서쪽으로 가다)) sun (노을을 말함). Then we'll be sure to have good weather to-morrow."

Maya made off quickly. She couldn't bear to stay and see the mosquito hurt the sleeping child. And how could she do this thing ((쏘는 것) (벌은 침을 쏘면 죽는데 모기는 죽지 않으니까)) and not perish (죽다)? Hadn't Cassandra said: "If you sting a human being, you will die?"

Maya still remembered every detail of this **incident** (사건)

with the child and the mosquito, but her craving(갈망, 열망) to know human beings well had not been **still**ed(가라앉히다). She made up her mind to be bolder and never stop trying until she had reached her goal.

At last Maya's longing to know human beings was to be satisfied, and in a way far, far lovelier and more wonderful than she had dreamed.

Once, on a warm evening, having gone to sleep earlier than usual, she woke up suddenly in the middle of the night—something that had never happened to her before. When she opened her eyes, her astonishment was indescribable(형언할 수 없는): her little bedroom was all **steep**ed(담그다, 잠그다) in a quiet bluish radiance(빛, 광휘). It came down through the entrance, and the entrance itself shone as if hung with a silver-blue curtain.

Maya did not dare to budge(움직이다) at first, though not because she was frightened. No. Somehow, along with the light came a rare, lovely peacefulness(평화로움), and outside her room the air was filled with a sound finer, more harmonious(조화된) than any music she had ever heard. After a time she rose timidly, awed(외경심을 느끼게 하다) by the glamour(황홀한 매력) and the strangeness of it all, and looked out. The whole world seemed to lie under the **spell**(마법, 주문) of an **enchantment**(마법을 걸기). Everything was sparkling (불꽃을 내는) and glittering in pure silver. The trunks of the birch-trees, the slumbering (자는) leaves were overlaid (overlay (온통 얇게 뒤덮다)의 과거분사) with silver. The grass, which from her height seemed to lie under delicate veils (베일, 면사포), was set (설치된) with a thousand pale pearls (진주). All things near and far, the silent distances, were **shroud**ed (덮다, 덮어 가리다) in this soft, bluish sheen (광택, 광휘).

"This must be the night," Maya whispered and folded (포개다) her hands.

High up in the heavens, partly veiled by the leaves of a beech-tree, hung a full clear disk (둥근 판) of silver, from which the radiance poured down that beautified the world. And then Maya saw countless bright, sharp little lights surrounding (둘러싼) the moon in the heavens—oh, so still and beautiful, unlike any shining things she had ever seen before. To think she beheld (보았다) the night, the moon, and the stars—the wonders, the lovely wonders (경이, 놀라움) of the night! She had heard of them but never believed in them. It was almost too much (너무나 대단한 것이었다).

Then the sound rose again, the strange night sound that must have awakened (깨우다) her. It came from nearby, filling the welkin (하늘, 창공), a soaring (높이 솟는(soar 높이 솟다)) chirp with a silvery ring (울림) that matched (어울리다) the silver on the trees and leaves and grass and seemed to come rilling (시내처럼 흐르다) down from the moon on the beams(빛) of silver light.

Maya looked about for the source(원천, 근원), in vain; in the mysterious drift(표류) of light and shadow it was difficult to make out(분간하다) objects in clear outline(윤곽), everything was **drape**d(싸다, 걸치다) so mysteriously; and yet everything showed up true and in such heroic(영웅적인) beauty.

Her room could keep her no longer; out she had to fly into this new splendor, the night splendor.

"The good Lord(하나님) will take care of me," she thought, "I am not **bent**(향한, 결심한) upon wrong."(내가 나쁜 것을 하려고 하지 않으니까)

As she was about to fly off through the silver light to her favorite meadow, now lying full under the moon, she saw a winged creature alight(내리다) on a beech-tree leaf not far away. Scarcely(~하자마자(when, before)) alighted, it raised its head to the moon, lifted its narrow wings, and drew the edge of one against the other, for all the world as though it were playing on a violin. And sure enough, the sound came, the silvery chirp that filled the whole moonlit world with melody(선율).

"Exquisite," whispered Maya, "heavenly(천국의), heavenly, heavenly."

She flew over to the leaf. The night was so mild and warm that she did not notice it was cooler than by day. When she touched the leaf, the chirper (찍찍 우는 벌레) broke off (그만 두었다) playing abruptly (갑작스럽게), and to Maya it seemed as if there had never been such a stillness before, so profound (깊은) was the **hush** (조용함) that followed. It was uncanny (기괴한, 불가사의한). Through the dark leaves **filter**ed (투과시키다) the light, white and cool.

"Good night," said Maya, politely, thinking "good night" was the greeting for the night like "good morning" for the morning. "Please excuse me for interrupting, but the music you make is so fascinating (매혹적인) that I had to find out where it came from."

The chirper stared at Maya, wide-eyed.

"What sort of a crawling creature are you?" it asked after some moments had passed. "I have never met one like you before."

"I am not a crawling insect. I am Maya, of the nation of bees."

"Oh, of the nation of bees. Indeed... you live by day, don't you? I have heard of your race from the hedgehog (고슴도치). He told me that in the evening he eats the dead bodies that are thrown out of your hive."

"Yes," said Maya, with a faint (약한) chill (기분 나쁨, 불쾌함, 냉기) of apprehension (걱정, 염려), "that's so; Cassandra told me about him; she heard of him from the sentinels(보초). He comes when twilight falls and snouts(주둥이로 파다, 주둥이) in the grass looking for dead bodies.—But do you associate(사귀다) with the hedgehog? Why, he's an awful brute."

"I don't think so. We tree-crickets get along with him splendidly. We call him Uncle. Of course he always tries to catch us, but he never succeeds(성공하다), so we have great fun teasing(tease 놀리다) him. Everybody has to live, doesn't he? Just so he doesn't live off(폐를 끼치다) me, what do I care?"

Maya shook her head. She didn't agree. But not caring to insult(모욕하다) the cricket by contradicting(contradict 이의를 제기하다), she changed the subject(주제).

"So you're a tree-cricket?"

"Yes, a snowy(눈 같은, 눈 같이 흰) tree-cricket.—But I must play, so please don't keep me any longer. It's full moon(보름달), a wonderful night. I must play."

"Oh, do make an **exception**(예외) this once. You play all the time.—Tell me about the night."

"A midsummer night is the loveliest in the world," answered the cricket. "It fills the heart with rapture(큰 기쁨).—But what my music doesn't tell you I shan't be able to explain. Why need everything be explained? Why know everything? We poor creatures can find out only the tiniest bit about existence(존재). Yet we can feel the glory of the whole wide world." And the cricket set up its happy silvery **strum**ming(가볍게 치다, 퉁기다). Heard from close by, where Maya sat, the music was overpowering(감동시키다, 압도하다) in its loudness(큰 소리).

The little bee sat quite still in the blue summer night listening and musing deeply about life and creation(창조).

Silence fell. There was a faint whirr(윙 소리), and Maya saw the cricket fly out into the moonlight.

"The night makes one feel sad," she reflected.

Her flowery meadow drew(끌었다) her now. She flew off.

At the edge of the brook stood the tall irises brokenly(들쭉날쭉, 부서져) reflected(반사되다) in the running water. A glorious sight. The moonlight was whirled(소용돌이 치다) along in the braided(꼰; braid 머리카락 등을 땋다) current(강의 흐름), the wavelets(잔물결) winked and whispered, the irises seemed (물이 흘러갈 때 돌 등에 부딪쳐 머리카락을 꼰 모습처럼 보이는 것을 말함) to lean(기대다) over asleep. "Asleep from sheer delight," thought the little bee. She dropped down(내렸다) on a blue petal in the full light of the moon and could not take her eyes from the living waters of the brook, the quivering(떨리는) flash(반짝임), the flashing come and go of countless sparks. On the bank(강둑) opposite(반대의), the birch-trees glittered as if hung with the stars.

"Where is all that water flowing to?" she wondered. "The cricket is right. We know so little about the world.”

Of a sudden a fine little voice rose in song from the flower of an iris close beside her, ringing like a pure, clear bell, different from any earthly sound that Maya knew. Her heart **throb**bed(고동치다), she held her breath(숨을 죽였다).

“Oh, what is going to happen? What am I going to see now?”

The iris swayed gently. One of the petals curved in at the edge, and Maya saw a tiny snow-white human hand holding on to the flower’s rim(가장자리) with its wee little fingers. Then a small blond(금빛의) head arose, and then a delicate **luminous**(빛나는) body in white garments(옷). A human being in miniature(축소 모형) was coming up out of the iris.

Words cannot tell Maya’s awe and rapture. She sat rigid(굳은).

The tiny being climbed to the edge of the blossom,

lifted its arms up to the moonlight, and looked out into the bright shining night with a smile of bliss(더 없는 기쁨) lighting up its face. Then a faint quiver shook its luminous body, and from its shoulders two wings unfolded(펼치다), whiter than the moonlight, pure as snow, rising above its blond head and reaching down to its feet. How lovely it was, how exquisitely lovely. Nothing that Maya had ever seen compared with (~와 비교하여) it in loveliness.

Standing there in the moonlight, holding its hands up to heaven, the luminous little being lifted (소리를 높이다) its voice again and sang. The song rang out in the night, and Maya understood the words.

My home is Light. The crystal bowl (속이 오목한 그릇)
Of Heaven's blue, I love it so!
Both Death and Life will change, I know,
But not my soul, my living soul.
My soul is that which breathes anew (새로이)
From all of loveliness and grace;
And as it flows from God's own face,
It flows from His creations, too.

Maya burst into sobs (흐느낌). What it was that made her so sad and yet so happy, she could not have told.

The little human being turned around.

"Who is crying?" he asked in his chiming (아름다운 소리의) voice.

chime (초인종 등으로) 아름다운 소리를 내다

"It's only me," stammered Maya. "Excuse me for

interrupting you."

"But why are you crying?"

"I don't know. Perhaps just because you are so beautiful. Who are you? Oh, do tell me, if I am not asking too much. You are an angel, aren't you? You must be."

"Oh, no," said the little creature, quite serious. "I am only a sprite (요정), a flower-sprite.—But, dear little bee, what are you doing out here in the meadow so late at night?"

The sprite flew over to a curving iris blade beside Maya and regarded (유심히 보다) her long and kindly from his swaying perch in the moonlight.

Maya told him all about herself, what she had done, what she knew, and what she longed for. And while she spoke, his eyes never left her, those large dark eyes glowing in the white fairy face under the golden hair that ever and anon (이따금) shone like silver in the moonlight.

When she finished he stroked (가볍게 쓰다듬다) her head and looked at her so warmly and lovingly that the little bee, beside herself (제정신이 아닌) with joy, had to lower (낮추다) her gaze.

"We sprites," he explained, "live seven nights, but

we must stay in the flower in which we are born, else we die at dawn."

Maya opened her eyes wide in terror.

"Then hurry, hurry! Fly back into your flower!"

The, sprite shook his head sadly.

"Too late.—But listen. I have more to tell you. Most of us sprites are glad to leave our flowers never to return, because a great happiness is connected (연결된) with our leaving. We are endowed with ([endow A with B] 〈신 등이〉 〈A(사람)에게 B(재능, 자질, 권리 등)를〉 주다, 부여하다) a remarkable (범상치 않은, 진기한) power: before we die, we can **fulfill** (이루다, 성취하다) the dearest wish of the first creature we meet. It is when we make up our minds seriously to leave the flower for the purpose of making someone happy that our wings grow."

"How wonderful!" cried Maya. "I'd leave the flower too, then. It must be lovely to fulfill another person's wish." That she was the first being whom the sprite on his flight from the flower had met, did not occur (생각이 떠오르다, 일어나다) to her. "And then—must you die?"

The sprite nodded, but not sadly this time.

"We live to see the dawn (새벽) still (여전히)," he said, "but when the dew falls, we are drawn into the fine cobwebby (거미집 같은) veils (장막) that float above the grass and the flowers of the meadows. Haven't you often noticed that the veils shine white as though a light were inside them? It's the sprites, their wings and their garments. When the light rises we change into dew- drops. The plants drink us and we become a part of their growing and blooming until in time we rise again as sprites from out their flowers."

"Then you were once another sprite?" asked Maya, tense(긴장한), breathless with interest.

The earnest eyes said yes.

"But I have forgotten my earlier(더 먼저의) existence. We forget(잊다) everything in our flower-sleep."

"Oh, what a lovely fate!"

"It is the same as that of all earthly creatures, when you really come to think of it, even if it isn't always flowers out of which they wake up from their sleep of death(죽음). But we won't talk of that to-night."

"Oh, I'm so happy!" cried Maya.

"Then you haven't got a wish? You're the first person I've met, you know, and I possess(가지다) the power to grant(주다) your dearest(가장 절실한) wish."

"I? But I'm only a bee. No, it's too much. It would be too great a joy. I don't deserve it, I don't deserve that you should be so good to me."

"No one deserves the good and the beautiful. The

good and the beautiful come to us like the sunshine."

Maya's heart beat stormily (세차게). Oh, she did have a wish, a burning wish, but she didn't dare confess it. The elf seemed to guess; he smiled so you couldn't keep anything a secret from him.

"Well?" He stroked his golden hair off his pure forehead.

"I'd like to know human beings at their best and most beautiful," said the little bee. She spoke quickly and hotly. She was afraid she would be told that so great a wish could not be granted.

But the sprite drew himself up, his expression was serious and serene (평온한), his eyes shone with confidence (신뢰, 신임). He took Maya's trembling hand and said:

"Come. We'll fly together. Your wish shall be granted."

CHAPTER 11

WITH THE SPRITE

And so Maya and the flower-sprite started off together in the bright mid-summer night, flying low over the blossomy meadow. His white reflection (비친 그림자) crossing the brook shone as though a star were gliding through the water.

How happy the little bee was to confide (맡기다, 비밀을 털어 놓다) herself to this gracious being! Whatever he were to do, wherever he were to lead her would be good and right, she felt. She would have liked to ask him a thousand questions had she dared.

As they were passing between a double row of high poplar (포플러)-trees, something whirred above them; a dark moth(나방), as big and strong as a bird, crossed their way.

"One moment, wait one moment, please," the sprite called.

Maya was surprised to see how readily the moth responded(반응하다).

All three alighted on a high poplar branch, from which there was a far view out upon the **tranquil**(고요한), moonlit(달빛에 비친) landscape. The quaking(quake 떨다) leaves whispered delicately. The moth, perching directly opposite Maya in the full light of the moon, slowly lifted his spread wings and dropped them again, softly, as if gently fanning(부채질 하다)—fanning a cool breath upon someone. Broad, **diagonal**(대각선의) **stripe**(줄무늬)s of a gorgeous(화려한) bright blue marked(표시하다) his wings, his black head was covered as with dark velvet(벨벳 천 같은 것), his face was like a strangely mysterious mask(가면), out of which glowed a pair of dark eyes. How wonderful were the creatures of the night! A little cold shiver ran through Maya, who felt she was dreaming the strangest dream of her life.

"You are beautiful," she said to the moth, "beautiful, really." She was awed and solemn(엄숙한).

"Who is your companion?" the moth asked the sprite.

"A bee. I met her just as I was leaving my flower."

The moth seemed to realize what that meant. He looked at Maya almost enviously.

"You fortunate(운 좋은) creature!" he said in a low, serious, musing(생각에 잠기는) tone, shaking his head to and fro.

"Are you sad?" asked Maya out of the warmth of her heart.

The moth shook his head.

"No, not sad." His voice sounded friendly and grateful(상쾌한), and he gave Maya such a kind look that she would have liked to strike up(친교를 맺다) a friendship(우정) with him then and there(곧장, 그 때 그 자리에서).

"Is the bat still abroad(바깥에, 외국에), or has he gone to rest?" This was the question for which the sprite had stopped the moth.

"Oh, he's gone to rest long ago. You want to know, do you, on account of(~때문에) your companion?"

The sprite nodded(고개를 끄덕이다). Maya was dying(죽을 정도로 하고 싶은) to find out what a bat was, but the sprite seemed to be in a hurry. With a charming gesture of restlessness(안절부절) he tossed his shining hair back from his forehead.

"Come, Maya," he said, "we must hurry. The night is so short."

"Shall I carry you part of the way?" asked the

moth.

The sprite thanked him but **decline**(거절하다)d. "Some other time!" he called.

"Then it will be never," thought Maya as they flew away, "because at dawn the flower-sprite must die."

The moth remained on the leaf looking after them until the glimmer(희미한 빛) of the fairy garments grew smaller and smaller and finally sank(가라 앉았다) into the depths of the blue distance(거리). Then he turned his face slowly and **survey**(바라보다, 조사하다)ed his great dark wings with their broad blue stripes. He sank into revery(reverie 몽상).

"So often I have heard that I am gray and ugly," he said to himself, "and that my dress is not to be compared with the superb robes(자락이 길고 넉넉한 옷) of the butterfly. But the little bee saw only what is beautiful in me.—And she asked me if I was sad. I wonder whether I am or not.—No, I am not sad," he decided, "not now."

Meanwhile Maya and the flower-sprite flew through the dense(울창한, 밀집한) shrubbery(관목) of a garden. The glory of it in the dimmed(희미한) moonlight was beyond the power of mortal(죽어야 할 운명의, 인간의) lips to say. An intoxicatingly(취할 만큼) sweet cool breath(숨, 입김, 호흡) of dew and slumbering flowers transformed(바꾸다) all things into unutterable(말로 나타낼 수 없는) blessings(은혜). The lilac(라일락 색의) grapes(꽃송이, 포도) of the acacias(아카시아)

sparkled in freshness(새로움), the June rose-tree looked like a small blooming heaven hung with red lamps, the white stars of the jasmine glowed palely(창백하게), sadly, and poured out(쏟아 부었다) their perfume as if, in this one hour, to make a gift(재능, 선물) of their all.

Maya was dazed(멍해지게 하다). She pressed the sprite's hand and looked at him. A light of bliss shone from his eyes.

"Who could have dreamed of this!" whispered the little bee.

Just then she saw something that sent a pang(상심, 비통) through her.

"Oh," she cried, "look! A star has fallen! It's **stray**ing(길에서 벗어나다) about and can't find its way back to its place in the sky."

"That's a firefly(개똥벌레)," said the flower-sprite, without a smile.

Now, in the midst(한복판, 중앙) of her amazement, Maya realized for the first time why the sprite seemed so dear and kind. He never laughed at her ignorance(모름); on the contrary, he helped her when she went wrong.

"They are odd(이상한) little creatures," the sprite continued. "They carry their own light about with them on warm summer nights and enliven(활기 띠게 하다) the dark under the shrubbery where the moonlight doesn't shine through. So firefly can keep **tryst** ((연인끼리의) 만남, 밀회) with firefly even in the dark. Later, when we come to the human beings, you will make the acquaintance of one of them."

"Why?" asked Maya.

"You'll soon see."

By this time they had reached an **arbor** (나무 그늘의 휴식 장소, 정자) completely overgrown with jasmine and woodbine (인동덩굴). They descended (내려가다) almost to the ground. From close by, within the arbor, came the sound of faint whispering (속삭임). The flower-sprite beckoned (손짓하다) to a firefly.

"Would you be good enough," he asked, "to give us a little light? We have to push through these dark leaves here; we want to get to the inside of the jasmine-arbor."

"But your glow is much brighter than mine."

"I think so, too," put in Maya, more to hide her excitement than anything else.

"I must wrap (싸다) myself up in a leaf," explained the sprite, "else the human beings would see me and be frightened. We sprites appear to human beings only in their dreams."

"I see," said the firefly. "I am at your service. I will

do what I can.—Won't the great beast with you hurt me?"

The sprite shook his head no, and the firefly believed him.

The sprite now took a leaf and wrapped himself in it; the gleam of his white garments was completely hidden. Then he picked a little bluebell from the grass and put it on his shining head like a helmet(헬멧). The only bit of him left exposed(드러난) was his face, which was so small that surely no one would notice it. He asked the firefly to perch on his shoulder and with its wing to dim(흐릿하게 하다) its lamp on the one side so as to(~하기 위해) keep the **dazzle**(눈부심) out of his eyes.

"Come now," he said, taking Maya's hand. "We had better climb up right here."

The little bee was thinking of something the sprite had said, and as they **clamber**(기어오르다)ed up the vine, she asked:

"Do human beings dream when they sleep?"

"Not only then(그 때 뿐만 아니라(잘 때 뿐만 아니라)). They dream sometimes even when they are awake(깨어 있는). They sit with their bodies a little limp(축 늘어진), their heads bent a little forward, and their eyes searching the distance, as if to see into the very heavens. Their dreams are always lovelier than life. That's why we appear to them in their dreams."

The sprite now laid his tiny finger on his lips, bent(구부렸다) aside a small blooming sprig(작은 가지) of jasmine, and gently pushed Maya ahead.

"Look down," he said softly, "you'll see what you have been wishing to see."

The little bee looked and saw two human beings sitting on a bench in the shadows cast(던지다(cast-cast-cast)) by the moonlight—a boy and a girl, the girl with her head leaning on the boy's shoulder, and the boy holding his arm around the girl as if to protect(보호하다) her. They sat in complete stillness(고요함), looking wide-eyed into the night. It was as quiet as if they had both gone to sleep. Only from a distance came the chirping of the crickets, and slowly, slowly the moonlight drifted(떠다니다) through the leaves.

Maya, transported(황홀하게 하다) out of herself, gazed into the girl's face. Although it looked pale and wistful(생각에 잠긴), it seemed to be transfused(주입하다, 스며들게 하다) by the hidden radiance of a great happiness. Above her large eyes lay(있었다) golden hair, (그녀의 큰 눈 위로 황금빛의 머리카락이 있었다) like the golden hair of the sprite, and upon it rested the heavenly sheen(광휘) of the midsummer night. From her red lips, slightly parted(갈라진(part 가르다, 찢다)), came a breath of rapture and melancholy, as if she wanted to offer everything that was hers to the man by her side for his happiness.

And now she turned to him, pulled his head down, and whispered a magical something that brought a smile to his face such as Maya thought no earthly being could wear. In his eyes gleamed a happiness and a **vigor** as if the whole big world were his to own, and suffering and misfortune were **banish**ed forever from the face of the earth.

Maya somehow had no desire to know what he said to the girl in reply. Her heart quivered as though the ecstasy that **emanate**d from the two human beings was also hers.

"Now I have seen the most glorious thing that my eyes will ever behold," she whispered to herself. "I know now that human beings are most beautiful when they are in love."

How long Maya stayed behind the leaves without stirring, lost in looking at the boy and girl, she did not know. When she turned round, the firefly's lamp had been **extinguish**ed, the sprite was gone. Through the doorway of the arbor far across the country on the distant horizon showed a narrow **streak** of red.

수평선에서 좁은 빨간 줄(해가 뜨면서)을 보여 주었다

CHAPTER 12

ALOIS, LADYBIRD AND POET

The sun was risen high above the tops of the beech-trees when Maya awoke in her woodland retreat (은퇴처(Maya의 집을 말함), 철수). In the first moments, the moonlight, the chirping of the cricket, the midsummer night meadow, the lovely sprite, the boy and the girl in the arbor, all seemed the perishing (죽는, 멸망하는) fancies (공상들) of a delicious dream. Yet here it was almost mid-day; and she remembered (기억하다) ((동명사가 목적어이면 과거에 한 것을 기억, to 부정사가 목적어이면 미래에 할 일을 기억)) slipping back into her chamber (방) in the chill of dawn. So it had all been real, she had spent ((시간을)보냈다) the night with the flower-sprite and had seen the two human beings, with their arms round each other, in the arbor of woodbine and jasmine.

The sun outside was glowing hot on the leaves, a

warm wind was stirring, and Maya heard the mixed chorus of thousands of insects. Ah, what these knew, and what she knew! So proud was she of the great thing that had happened to her that she couldn't get out to the others fast enough; she thought they must read it in her very looks.

But in the sunlight everything was the same as ever. Nothing was changed; nothing recalled the blue moonlit night. The insects came, said how-doyou-do, and left; yonder, the meadow was a scene of bustling activity; the insects, birds and butterflies hopped, flew and flitted in the hot flickering air around the tall, gay midsummer flowers.

Sadness fell upon Maya. There was no one in the world to share her joys and sorrows. She couldn't make up her mind to fly over and join the others in the meadow. No, she would go to the woods. The woods were serious and solemn. They **suit**ed her mood.

How many mysteries and marvels lie hidden in the dim depths of the woods, no one suspects who hurries unobservant along the beaten tracks. You must bend aside the branches of the underbrush, or lean down and peep between the blackberry briars through the tall grasses and across the thick moss(이끼). Under the shaded(그늘진) leaves of the plants, in holes in the ground and tree-trunks, in the **decay**ing(썩는(decay 썩다)) bark of **stump**s(그루터기, 밑동), in the curl(돌돌 감긴 것) and twist(꼬인 것) of the roots that coil(휘감기다, 굽이치다) on the ground like serpents(뱀), there is an active(활동적인, 분주한), multiform(다양한, 많은 형태의) life by day and by night, full of joys and dangers, struggles(분투) and sorrows and pleasures.

Maya **divine**d(추측하다, 예언하다, 신의) only a little of this as she flew low between the dark-brown trunks under the leafy roof of green. She followed a narrow trail in the grass, which made a clear path through thicket(덤불) and clearing(빈터). Now and then the sun seemed to disappear behind clouds, so deep was the shade under the high **foliage**(전체 잎) and in the close(빽빽한) shrubbery; but soon she was flying again through a bright shimmer of gold and green above the broad-leaved miniature(작은, 축소된) forests of bracken(고사리, 덤불) and blackberry.

After a long stretch(거리, 범위) the woods opened their columned(기둥이 있는) and over-arched(아치형으로 구부러진) **portal**s(입구); before Maya's eyes lay a wide field(들판) of **grain**(낟알, 곡물, 곡식) in the golden sunshine. Butter-fly-weed(국화과의 꽃) flamed(빛나다) on the grassy borders(가장자리). She alighted on the branch of a birch-tree at the edge of the field and gazed upon the sea of gold that spread out endlessly(끝없이) in the **tranquillity**(고요, 평안) of the **placid**(조용한) day. It rippled(잔물결을 일으키다) softly under the shy summer breeze, which blew ((바람이) 불었다) gently (부드럽게) so as not to disturb (어지럽히다) the peace of the lovely world.

Under the birch-tree a few small brown butterflies, using the butterfly-weed for corners (구석), were playing puss-in-the-corner (집뺏기 숨바꼭질), a favorite game with butterfly-children. Maya watched them a while (잠시 동안).

"It must be lots of fun," she thought, "and the children in the hive might be taught to play it, too. The cells would do for corners.—But Cassandra, I suppose, wouldn't permit it. She's so strict (엄격한)."

Ah, now Maya felt sad again. Because she had thought of home. And she was about to drift off into homesick revery (몽상) when she heard someone beside her say:

"Good morning. You're a beast, it seems to me."

Maya turned with a start.

"No," she said, "decidedly (명확하게, 단연코) not."

There sitting on her leaf was a little polished (광택이 나는) terra-cotta (갈색이 섞인 붉은색의, 테라코타[brownish-red clay(진흙)]) half-sphere (구) with seven black dots on its cupola (둥근 지붕, 반구(半球) 천장) of a back (등), a minute (미세한) black head and bright little eyes. Peeping from under the dotted dome and supporting it as best they could Maya **detect**ed (간파하다, 탐지하다) thin legs fine as threads. In spite of his queer figure, she somehow took a great liking to the **stout**(뚱뚱한) little fellow; he had distinct(독특한) charm.

"May I ask who you are? I myself am Maya of the nation of bees."

"Do you mean to insult(모욕하다) me? You have no reason(이유) to."

"But why should I? I don't know you, really I don't." Maya was quite upset.

"It's easy to say you don't know me.—Well, I'll **jog**(기억을 불러일으키게 하다, 조깅하다) your memory(기억). Count(세다)." And the little **rotundity**(구모양, 원형, 통통함) began to wheel round(돌다) slowly.

"You mean I'm to count your dots?"

"Yes, if you please."

"Seven," said Maya.

"Well?—Well? You still don't know. All right then, I'll tell you. I'm called exactly according to(~에 따르면) what you counted. The **scientific**(과학의) name of our family is Septempunctata(칠성무당벌레). Septem is Latin for seven, punctata is Latin for dots, points, you see. Our common name is ladybird(무당벌레), my own name is Alois, I am a poet(시인) by profession(직업). You know our common(일반) name, of course."

Maya, afraid of hurting Alois' feelings, didn't dare

to say no.

"Oh," said he, "I live by the sunshine, by the peace of the day, and by the love of mankind(인류)."

"But don't you eat, too?" asked Maya, quite astonished.

"Of course. Plant-lice(진딧물들(lice는 louse(이)의 복수)). Don't you?"

"No. That would be—that is..."

"Is what? Is what?"

"Not—usual," said Maya shyly.

"Of course, of course!" cried Alois, trying to raise one shoulder, but not succeeding, on account of the firm set of his dome(반구(등껍질을 말함)). "As a bourgeoise(bourgeois (부르주아)의 여성형, 유산계급, 중산계급) you would, of course, do only what is usual(보통의). We poets would not get very far that way.—Have you time?"

"Why, yes," said Maya.

"Then I'll recite(낭독하다) you one of my poems(시). Sit real still and close your eyes, so that nothing **distract**s(주의를 딴 데로 돌리다) your attention. The poem is called Man's Finger, and is about a personal experience. Are you listening?"

"Yes, to every word."

"Well, then:

"'Since you did not do me wrong,

That you found me, doesn't matter.

You are rounded, you are long;
Up above you wear a flatter,
Pointed, polished sheath or platter
Which you move as swift as light,
But below you're fastened tight!'"

"Well?" asked Alois after a short pause. There were tears in his eyes and a quaver in his voice.

"Man's Finger gripped me very hard," replied Maya in some embarrassment. She really knew much lovelier poems.

"How do you find the form?" Alois questioned with a smile of fine melancholy. He seemed to be overwhelmed by the effect he had produced.

"Long and round. You yourself said so in the poem."

"I mean the **artistic** form, the form of my **verse**."

"Oh—oh, yes. Yes, I thought it was very good."

"It is, isn't it!" cried Alois. "What you mean to say is that Man's Finger may be **rank**ed among the best poems you know of, and one must go way back in **literature** before one comes across anything like it. The **prime** **requisite** in art is that it should contain something new, which is what most poets forget. And bigness, too. Don't you agree with me?"

"Certainly," said Maya, "I think..."

"The firm(확고한) belief(믿음) you express(표현하다) in my importance(중요함) as a poet really overwhelms(압도하다) me. I thank you.—But I must be going now, for **solitude**(고독) is the poet's pride. Farewell."

"Farewell," echoed(되풀이하여 말하다, 울려 퍼지다) Maya, who really didn't know just what the little fellow had been after.

"Well," she thought, "he knows. Perhaps he's not full grown yet; he certainly isn't large." She looked after him, as he hastened(서둘러 ~하다) up the branch. His wee legs were scarcely visible; he looked as though he were moving on low rollers(굴림대, 롤러).

Maya turned her gaze away, back to the golden field of grain over which the butterflies were playing. The field and the butterflies gave her ever so much more pleasure than the poetry(시) of Alois, ladybird and poet.

CHAPTER 13

THE FORTRESS

How happily the day had begun and how miserably (비참하게) it was to end!

Before the horror swept (휩쓸었다) upon her, Maya had formed a very remarkable (진기한) acquaintance. It was in the afternoon near a big old water-butt (큰 통). She was sitting amid the scented elder (딱총나무) blossoms, which lay mirrored (비추어지다) in the placid (평온한) dark surface of the butt, and a robin redbreast was warbling (warble 지저귀다) overhead, so sweetly and merrily (즐겁게) that Maya thought it was a shame (창피), a crying shame that she, a bee, could not make friends with the charming songsters (가수, 우는 새). The trouble was, they were too big and ate you up.

She had hidden herself in the heart (중심부) of the elder

blossoms and was listening and blinking under the pointed(날카로운) darts(던지는 화살) of the sunlight (햇볕이 눈을 부시게 한다는 표현), when she heard someone beside her sigh. Turning round she saw—well, now it really was the strangest of all the strange creatures she had ever met. It must have had at least a hundred legs along each side of its body—so she thought at first glance. It was about three times her size, and slim(가는), low(낮은, 납작한), and wingless.

"For goodness sake! Mercy on me!" Maya was quite startled(놀란). "You must certainly be able to run!"

The stranger gave her a pondering(숙고하다, 곰곰이 생각하다) look.

"I doubt it," he said. "I doubt it. There's room(여지) for improvement(개량, 개선). I have too many legs. You see, before all my legs can be set in motion(움직임), too much time is lost. I didn't use to realize this, and often wished I had a few more legs. But God's will be done(하나님이 한 것이죠(하나님의 뜻이죠)).—Who are you?"

Maya introduced herself. The other one nodded and moved some of his legs.

"I am Thomas of the family of millepeds(노래기) (mill은 많다, pede는 '다리'라는 뜻임). We are an old race, and we arouse(일으키다) admiration and astonishment in all parts of the globe(지구, 둥근 공). No other animals can boast(자랑하다) anything like our number of legs. Eight is their limit(한계), so far as I know."

"You are tremendously (엄청나게) interesting. And your color is so queer. Have you got a family?"

"Why, no! Why should I? What good would a family do me? We millepeds crawl out of our eggs; that's all. If we can't stand on our own feet, who should?"

"Of course, of course," Maya observed (말하다) thoughtfully. "But have you no relations (친척)?"

"No, dear child. I earn (벌다) my living, and doubt (의심하다). I doubt."

"Oh! What do you doubt?"

"I was born doubting. I must doubt."

Maya stared at him in wide-eyed bewilderment (당혹, 당황). What did he mean, what could he possibly mean? She couldn't for the life of her (for the life of one 아무리 해도 (…않다)) make out, but she did not want to pry (비밀을 캐다, 엿보다) too curiously (호기심에서) into his private (사적인) affairs (일).

"For one thing," said Thomas after a pause, "for one thing I doubt whether you have chosen (choose (선택하다)의 과거분사) a good place to rest in. Don't you know what's over there in the big willow?"

"No."

"You see! I doubted right away if you knew. The city of the hornets (말벌) is over there."

Maya turned deathly (죽은 듯이) white and nearly fell off the elder blossoms. In a voice shaking with fright (경악, 겁), she asked just where the city was.

"Do you see that old nesting (둥지)-box for starlings (찌르레기), there in the shrubbery near the trunk of the willow-tree? It's so poorly placed that I doubted from the first whether starlings would ever move (이사하다) in. If a bird-house isn't set with its door facing (face 마주보다) the sunrise, every decent (고상한, 조심성 있는) bird will think twice before taking possession (소유, 가짐). Well, the hornets have **entrench**ed (침범하다, 참호를 파다) themselves in it. It's the biggest hornets' fortress (요새) in the country. You as a bee certainly ought to know of the place. Why, the hornets are brigands (강도, 약탈자) who lie in wait for you bees. So, at least, I have observed."

Maya scarcely heard what he was saying. There, showing clear against the green, she saw the brown walls of the fortress. She almost stopped breathing.

"I must fly away," she cried.

Too late! Behind her sounded a loud, mean laugh. At the same moment the little bee felt herself caught by the neck, so violently (격렬하게) that she thought her joints (관절) were broken. It was a laugh she would never forget, like a **vile** (역겨운, 몹시 나쁜) **taunt** (비웃음, 비꼼) out of hellish (지옥 같은) darkness. Mingling (mingle 섞이다) with it was another gruesome sound, the awful clanking of armor.

Thomas let go with all his legs at once and tumbled head over heels through the branches into the water-butt.

"I doubt if you get away alive," he called back. But the poor little bee no longer heard.

She couldn't see her **assailant**, her neck was caught in too firm a grip, but a gilt-sheathed arm passed before her eyes, and a huge head with dreadful pincers suddenly thrust itself above her face. She took it at first to belong to a gigantic wasp, but then realized that she had fallen into the clutches of a hornet. The black-and-yellow striped monster was surely four times her size.

Maya lost sight, hearing, speech; every **nerve** in her body went faint. At length her voice came back, and she screamed for help.

"Never mind, girlie," said the hornet in a honey-sweet tone that was sickening. "Never mind. It'll last until it's over." He smiled a **baleful** smile.

"Let go!" cried Maya. "Let me go! Or I'll sting you in your heart."

"In my heart right away? Very brave. But there's time for that later."

Maya went into a fury. **Summon**(불러일으키다, 호출하다)**ing** all her strength, she twisted(비틀다) herself around, uttered(소리를 내다) her shrill(날카로운) battle-cry, and directed(이끌다) her sting against the middle of the hornet's breast. To her amazement and horror, the sting, instead of piercing(pierce 뚫다) his breast, **swerve**(빗나가다)d on the surface. The brigand's armor was **impervious**(영향을 받지 않는, 통과시키지 않는).

Wrath(분노) gleamed(번득이다) in his eyes.

"I could bite your head off, little one, to punish(벌주다) you for your impudence(건방짐, 무례함). And I would, too, I would indeed, but for our queen. She prefers(좋아하다) fresh bees to(~보다) dead **carcasse**(시체)s. So a good soldier saves a juicy(즙이 많은) **morsel**(맛있는 음식, 음식물의 한 입) like you to bring to her alive."

The hornet, with Maya still in his grip, rose into the air and made directly for the fortress.

"This is too awful," thought the poor little bee. "No one can stand(참다, 견디다) this." She fainted(기절하다).

When she came to her senses(정신을 차렸다), she found herself in half darkness, in a **sultry**(무더운, 찌는 듯이 더운) **dusk**(어스름, 해질녘) **permeate**(투과하다, 퍼지다)d by a horrid, **pungent**(신랄한, 자극하는) smell. Slowly everything came back to her. A great **paralyzing**(마비시키는) sadness settled in her heart. She wanted to cry: the tears refused(거절하다) to come.

"I haven't been eaten up

yet, but I may be, any moment (언제든지)," she thought in a tremble (떨림).

Through the walls of her prison she caught the distinct (분명한) sound of voices, and soon she noticed that a little light filtered (스며나오다, 투과하다) through a narrow chink (갈라진 틈). The hornets make their walls, not of wax (밀랍) like the bees, but of a dry mass (덩어리) resembling (resemble 닮다) **porous** (다공성의, 구멍이 많은) grey paper. By the one thread (가느다란 선, 실) of light she managed bit by bit (점차) to make out her surroundings (주위). Horror of horrors! Maya was almost **congeal**ed (굳어지다) with fright: the floor was **strewn** (흩뿌려진, strew(흩뿌리다)의 과거분사) with the bodies of dead insects. At her very feet lay a little rose-beetle turned over on its back; to one side was the **skeleton** (골격) of a large locust (메뚜기) broken in two, and everywhere were the remains (나머지, 잔여물) of **slaughter**ed (죽이다, 살해하다) bees, their wings and legs and sheaths.

"Oh, oh, to think this had to happen to me," whimpered little Maya. She did not dare to stir (움직이다) the **fraction** (부분) of an inch and pressed (누르다, 밀다) herself shivering (떨다) into the farthest corner of this chamber of horrors.

Again she heard voices on the other side of the wall. **Impel**led (억지로 ~하게 하다) by mortal (지독한, 죽음의) fear (공포), she crept up to the chink and peeped through. What she saw was a vast (거대한) hall crowded (가득 찬) with hornets and magnificently (웅장하게) illuminated (빛을 받은) by a number of captive (붙잡힌) glow-worms (반딧불이). **Enthrone**d (왕좌에 앉다) in their midst sat the queen, who seemed to be holding an important council. Maya caught every word that was said.

If those glittering monsters had not inspired her with such unspeakable horror, she would have gone into raptures over their strength and magnificence. It was the first time she had had a good view of any of the race of brigands. Tigers they looked like, superb tigers of the insect world, with their tawny black-barred bodies. A shiver of awe ran through the little bee.

A sergeant-at-arms went about the walls of the hall ordering the glow-worms to give all the light they could; they must **strain** themselves to the utmost. He muttered his commands in a low voice, so as not to interrupt the **deliberation**s, and thrust at them with a long spear, hissing as he did so:

"Light up, or I'll eat you!"

Terrible the things that were done in the fortress of the hornets!

Then Maya heard the queen say:

"Very well, we shall **abide by** the arrangements we have made. To-morrow, one hour before dawn, the warriors will **assemble** and **sally forth** to the attack on the city of the bees in the castle park. The hive is to be

plunder(약탈하다)ed and as many prisoners(포로) taken as possible. He who captures(붙잡다) Queen Helen VIII and brings her to me alive will be **dub**(기사 작위를 주다 (어깨를 검으로 가볍게 두드려 기사 작위를 수여하다))bed a knight(기사). Go forth and be brave and victorious(승리의) and bring back rich **booty**(노획물, 약탈물).—The meeting is herewith(이것과 함께) adjourned(휴회하다). Sleep well, my warriors. I bid(명령하다, 인사하다) you good-night."

The queen-hornet rose from her throne(왕좌) and left the hall accompanied(~와 함께, 동반하여) by her body-guard(보디가드).

Maya nearly cried out loud.

"My country!" she sobbed, "my bees, my dear, dear bees!" She pressed her hands to her mouth to keep herself from screaming. She was in the depths of despair(절망). "Oh, would that I had died before I heard this. No one will warn my people. They will be attacked in their sleep and **massacre**(학살하다, 대량 학살)d. O God, perform(행하다) a miracle(기적), help me, help me and my people. Our need is great!"

In the hall the glow-worms were put out(불을 끄다) and **devour**(게걸스레 먹다)ed. Gradually(점차) the fortress was wrapped in a hush(고요함). Maya seemed to have been forgotten. A faint twilight crept into her cell(감방), and she thought she caught the strumming(가볍게 치다, 악기를 퉁기다) of the crickets' night song outside.—Was anything more horrible than this dungeon(지하 감옥) with its carcasses(시체) strewn(흩뿌려진) on the ground(땅, 지면)!

CHAPTER **14**

THE SENTINEL

Soon, however, the little bee's despair **yield**ed(양보하다, 내주다) to a definite(명백한) resolve(결심). It was as though she once more called to mind(기억하다) that she was a bee.

"Here I am weeping(울다) and wailing," she thought, "as if I had no brains(두뇌, 지능) and as if I were a weakling(허약자, 병약자). Oh, I'm not much of an honor to my people and my queen. They are in danger. I am doomed(죽을 운명의) anyhow. So since death is certain one way or another(어떻든지), I may as well be proud and brave and do everything I can to try to save them."

It was as though Maya had completely(완전히) forgotten the long time that had passed since she left her home. More strongly than ever she felt herself one of her people;

and the great responsibility (책임감) that suddenly **devolve**d (옮겨지다, 맡겨지다) upon her, through the knowledge of the hornets' plot (음모), filled her with fine courage and **determination** (결의).

"If my people are to **be vanquished** (패배하다(vanquish 무찌르다, 패배시키다)) and killed, I want to be killed, too. But first I must do everything in my power to save them."

"Long live my queen!" she cried.

"Quiet in there!" clanged (금속 등이 부딪치는 소리를 내다) harshly (귀에 거슬리게) from the outside. Ugh, what an awful voice!—The watchman (경비원) making his rounds (순찰, 한 회, 한 차례).—Then it was already late in the night.

As soon as the watchman's footsteps had died away (사라지다, 죽다(away)), Maya began to widen (넓히다) the chink through which she had peeped into the hall. It was easy to bite away the **brittle** (부서지기 쉬운) stuff (것, 물질) of the partition (칸막이), though it took some time before the opening was large enough to admit (들어가는 것을 허락하다) her body. At length, in the full knowledge (앎) that discovery (발견) would cost (값을 치르다) her her life (발견되면 그녀가 그녀의 목숨으로 값을 치러야 하는 것을 충분히 앎으로), she **squeeze**d (쑤셔 넣다) through into the hall. From remote (멀리 떨어진) depths of the fortress echoed the sound of loud snoring (코고는 소리).

The hall lay in a subdued (억제된) blue light that found its way in through the distant entrance (입구).

"The moonlight!" Maya said to herself. She began to creep cautiously toward the exit, **cower**ing (움츠리다) close (빽빽이) in the deep shadows of the walls, until she reached the high, narrow passageway that led from the hall to the opening through which the light shone. She heaved(한숨을 쉬다) a deep sigh. Far, far away glimmered a star.

"Liberty(자유)!" she thought.

The passageway(통로) was quite bright. Softly, stepping oh so very softly, Maya crept on. The portal(입구) came nearer and nearer.

"If I fly now," she thought, "I'll be out in one dash(돌진)." Her heart pounded(세차게 고동치다, 때리다) as if ready to burst(폭발하다).

But there in the shadow of the doorway stood a sentinel(보초) leaning against a column(기둥).

Maya stood still, rooted(한자리에 뿌리박다(꼼짝 않다)) to the spot(장소). **Vanish**(사라지다)ed all her hopes. Gone(가버렸다) the chance of escape. There was no getting by that **formidable**(무서운, 위협적인) figure(인물). What was she to do? Best go back where she had come from. But the sight of the giant in the doorway held her in a spell(매력, 마법). He seemed to be lost in(열중한) revery(몽상). He stood gazing out upon the moon-washed(달빛에 씻긴) landscape, his head tilted(기울어지다) slightly(약간) forward, his chin **prop**(괴다, 기대다)ped on his hand. How his golden cuirass(허리 갑옷) gleamed in the moonlight! Something in the way he stood there stirred the little bee's emotions(감정).

"He looks so sad," she thought. "How handsome

he is, how superbly(당당하게) he holds himself, how proudly his armor shines! He never removes(제거하다, 벗다) it, neither((~도 아니다)) by day nor((~아니다)) by night. He is always ready to rob(약탈하다) and fight and die..."

Little Maya quite forgot that this man was her enemy(적). Ah, how often the same thing had happened to her—that the goodness of her heart and her delight in beauty made her lose all sense of danger.

A golden dart(돌진, 짧은 화살) of light shot from the bandit(무법자, 강도)'s helmet. He must have turned his head.

"My God," whispered Maya, "this is the end of me!"

But the sentinel said quietly:

"Just come here, child."

"What!" cried Maya. "You saw me?"

"All the time, child. You bit(bite (깨물다)의 과거) a hole through the wall, then you crept along—crept along—**tuck**(쑤셔 넣다)ing yourself very neatly(깔끔하게) into the dark places—until you reached the spot where you're standing. Then you saw me, and you lost heart(용기를 잃었다). Am I right?"

"Yes," said Maya, "quite right." Her whole body shook with terror. The sentinel, then, had seen her the entire time. She remembered having heard how keen(예리한) were the senses of these clever **freebooter**(약탈자, 해적)s.

"What are you doing here?" he asked

good-humoredly(상냥하게).

Maya still thought he looked sad. His mind seemed to be far away and not to concern(염려하다, 걱정하다) itself with what was of such moment(중대사, 순간) to her.
(그녀에게 그토록 중대한 일을 그는 아무 염려하지 않는 것 같았다)

"I'd like to get out," she answered. "And I'm not afraid. I was just startled(놀란). You looked so strong and handsome(잘생긴), and your armor shone so. Now I'll fight you."

The sentinel, slightly astonished, leaned forward, and looked at Maya and smiled. It was not an ugly smile, and Maya experienced(경험하다) an entirely new feeling: the young warrior's smile seemed to exercise(영향을 미치다, 발휘하다, 운동하다) a mysterious power over her heart.

"No, little one," he said almost tenderly(부드럽게), "you and I won't fight. You bees belong to a powerful nation, but man for man we hornets are stronger(더 강한). To do single battle with a bee would be beneath our dignity(위엄). If you like you may stay here a little while and chat. But only a little while. Soon I'll have to wake the soldiers(병사) up; then, back to your cell you must go."

How curious(이상한)! The hornet's lofty(기품 있는, 아주 높은) friendliness **disarm**ed(마음을 누그러지게 하다, 무장을 해제하다) Maya more than anger or hate could have done. The feeling with which he inspired her was almost admiration (찬양, 감탄). With great sad eyes she looked up at her enemy, and **constrained** (강요당한(constrain 강요하다, 억압하다)), as always, to follow the **impulse**s (충동) of her heart, she said:

"I have always heard bad things about hornets. But you are not bad. I can't believe you're bad."

The warrior looked at Maya.

"There are good people and bad people everywhere," he said, gravely. "But you mustn't forget we are your enemies, and shall always remain your enemies."

"Must an enemy always be bad?" asked Maya. "Before, when you were looking out into the moonlight, I forgot that you were hard and dangerous. You seemed sad, and I have always thought that people who were sad couldn't possibly be wicked (사악한)."

The sentinel said nothing, and Maya continued more boldly (대담하게):

"You are powerful. If you want to, you can put me back in my cell, and I'll have to die. But you can also set me free—if you want to."

At this the warrior drew himself up (몸을 일으켰다). His armor clanked, and the arm he raised shone in the moonlight.

But the moonlight was turning dimmer (더 희미하게) in the

passageway. Was dawn coming already?

"You are right," he said. "I can. My people and my queen have **entrust**ed me with this power. My orders are that no bee who has set foot in this fortress shall leave it alive. I shall keep faith with my people."

After a pause he added softly as if to himself: "I have learned by bitter experience how faithlessness can hurt—when Loveydear forsook me..."

Little Maya was overcome. She did not know what to say. Ah, the same sentiments moved her, too—love of her own kind, loyalty to her people. Nothing to be done here but to use force or **strategy**. Each did his duty, and yet each remained an enemy to the other.

But hadn't the sentinel mentioned a name? Hadn't he said something about someone's having been unfaithful to him? Loveydear—why, she knew Loveydear—the beautiful dragon-fly who lived at the lakeside among the waterlilies.

Maya quivered with excitement. Here, perhaps, was her **salvation**. But she wasn't quite sure how much good her knowledge would be to her. So she said prudently(신중하게):

"Who is Loveydear, if I may ask?"

"Never mind, little one. She's not your affair, and she's lost to me forever. I shall never find her again."

"I know Miss Loveydear." Maya forced(억지로 ~하다) herself to put the utmost(최대의) indifference(무관심) into her tone. "She belongs to the family of dragon-flies and she's the loveliest lady of all."

A tremendous(엄청난) change came over the warrior. He seemed to have forgotten where he was. He leapt(뛰어올랐다) over to Maya's sides as if blown by a violent gust(돌풍).

"What! You know Loveydear? Tell me where she is. Tell me, right away."

"No."

Maya spoke quietly and firmly; she glowed with secret delight.

"I'll bite your head off if you don't tell." The warrior drew(접근했다) dangerously close.

"It will be bitten off anyhow. Go ahead(어서 해). I shan't **betray**(누설하다, 배신하다) the lovely dragon-fly. She's a close friend of mine... You want to imprison(투옥하다) her."

The warrior breathed hard. In the gathering(몰려오는) dawn Maya could see that his forehead was pale and his eyes tragic(매우 슬픈, 비극의) with the inner struggle(투쟁) he was waging(wage 전쟁 등을 하다).

"Good God!" he said wildly(미친 듯이). "It's time to rouse the soldiers.—No, no, little bee, I don't want to harm Loveydear. I love her, more dearly than my life. Tell me where I shall find her again."

Maya was clever. She purposely(일부러) hesitated before she said:

"But I love my life."

"If you tell me where Loveydear lives"—Maya could see that the sentinel spoke with difficulty and was trembling all over—"I'll set you free. You can fly wherever you want."

"Will you keep your word(약속을 지키다)?"

"My word of honor as a brigand," said the sentinel proudly.

Maya could scarcely speak. But, if she was to be in time to warn her people of the attack, every moment **count**ed(중요하다). Her heart **exult**ed(기뻐 날뛰다).

"Very well," she said, "I believe you. Listen, then. Do you know the ancient(오래된, 옛날의, 고대의) linden(보리수)-trees near the castle? Beyond them lies one meadow after another, and finally comes a big lake. In a **cove**(작은 만, 후미진 곳) at the south end where the brook empties(empty 흘러 들다, 비우다) into the lake the waterlilies(수련들) lie spread out on the water in the sunlight. Near them, in the rushes (골풀), is where Loveydear lives. You'll find her there every day at noon when the sun is high in the heavens."

The warrior had pressed both hands to his pale brow (이마). He seemed to be having a desperate (필사적인) struggle with himself.

"You're telling the truth," he said softly and groaned, whether from joy or pain it was impossible to tell. "She told me she wanted to go where there were floating (둥둥 떠다니다) white flowers. Those must be the flowers you speak of. Fly away, then. I thank you."

And actually he stepped aside from the entrance.

Day was breaking.

"A brigand keeps his word," he said.

Not knowing that Maya had overheard (엿듣다) the deliberations (협의, 토의, 신중함) in the council chamber, he told himself that one small bee more or less (전혀 ~않다, 다소, 얼마간) made little difference (차이). Weren't there hundreds of others?

"Good-by," cried Maya, breathless (숨가쁘게) with haste, and flew off without a word of thanks.

As a matter of fact, there was no time to spare (남겨두다).

CHAPTER **15**

THE WARNING

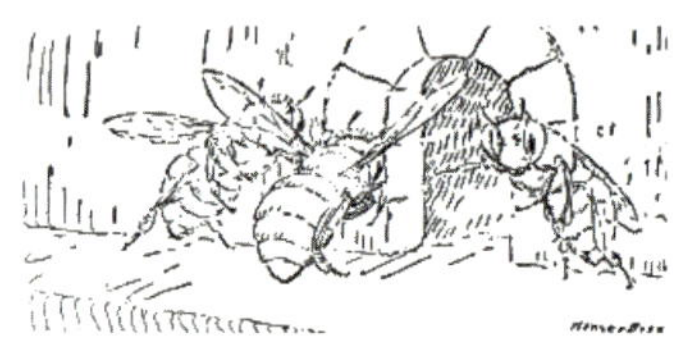

Little Maya summoned(불러일으키다, 호출하다) every bit of strength and will(의지) power she had left(남겨 두었다). Like a bullet(총알) shot(발사된) from the muzzle(총구, 주둥이) of a gun (bees can fly faster than most insects), she darted(날쌔게 움직이다) through the purpling dawn in a lightning(번개 같은) beeline(최단 코스, 직선 코스) for the woods, where she knew she would be safe for the moment and could hide herself away should the hornet regret(후회하다) having let her go and follow in **pursuit**(추적).

Gossamer(얇고 가벼운 천, 공중에 뜬 가는 거미줄) veils hung everywhere over the level(같은 높이의, 균등한) country(같은 높이로 얇은 베일(약한 안개)이 그 시골에 걸쳐있다), big drops fell from the trees on the dry leaves carpeting(온통 덮다) the ground, and the cold in the woods threatened(위협하다) to paralyze(마비시키다) little Maya's wings. No ray of the dawn had as yet found its way between the trees. The air was as hushed as if the sun had forgotten the earth, and all creatures had laid themselves to **eternal** (영원한) rest.

Maya, therefore, flew high up in the air. Only one thing mattered (중요하다)—to get back as quickly as strength and wits permitted to her hive, her people, her endangered (위험에 빠진(endanger 위험에 빠뜨리다)) home. She must warn her people. They must prepare against the attack which the terrible brigands had planned for that very morning. Oh, if only the nation of bees had the chance to arm (무장하다) and make ready its defenses (방어), it was well able to cope with (잘 대처하다) its stronger opponents (적). But a surprise (기습) assault (공격) at rising (일어나는) time! What if the queen and the soldiers were still asleep? The success of the hornets would then be assured (확실한, 보증된). They would take prisoners and give no quarter (살려주지 않다(give quarter 살려주다) quarter 항복자에 대한 자비). The butchery (학살) would be horrible.

Thinking of the strength and energy of her people, their readiness (준비) to meet death, their devotion (헌신) to their queen, the little bee felt a great wrath (분노) against their enemies the hornets. Her beloved (사랑하는) people! No sacrifice (희생) was too great for them. Little Maya's heart **swell**ed (넘치다, 부풀다) with the ecstasy (무아의 경지) of self-sacrifice (희생) and the **dauntless** (두려움을 모르는, 불굴의) courage of enthusiasm.

It was not easy for her to find her way over the woods. Long before she had ceased (그치다) to observe landmarks (경계표지)

as did the other bees, who had great distances to come back with their loads of nectar. She felt she had never flown as high before, the cold hurt, and she could scarcely (거의 ~할 수 없다) distinguish (구별하다) the objects below.

"What can I go by?" she thought. "No one thing stands out (두드러지다, 눈에 띄다). I shan't be able to reach my people and help them. Oh, oh! And here I had a chance to **atone** (보상하다, 벌충하다) for my **desertion** (도망, 탈주, 버림). What shall I do? What shall I do?"—Suddenly some secret force steered (조종하다) her in a certain direction. "What is pushing and pulling me? It must be homesickness guiding me back to my country." She gave herself up to the instinct (본능) and flew swiftly on. Soon, in the distance, looking like grey domes in the dim light of the dawn, showed the mighty lindens (보리수) of the castle park. She exclaimed with delight. She knew where she was. She dropped closer to the earth. In the meadows on one side hung the luminous (빛을 내는) wisps (한 조각) of fog, thicker here than in the woods. She thought of the flower-sprites who cheerfully died their early death inside the floating veils. That inspired her anew with confidence (자신감). Her anxiety (불안) disappeared. Let her people **spurn** (퇴짜놓다, 거절하다, 업신여기다) her from the kingdom, let the queen punish her for desertion, if only the bees were spared (살아남다, 면제되다) this dreadful **calamity** (재난, 불운) of the hornets' invasion (침입).

Close to the long stone wall shone the silver-fir (전나무) that shielded (가리다) the bee-city against the west wind. And there—she could see them distinctly now—were the red, blue, and green portals of her homeland (고향). The stormy pounding (박동, 뜀) of her heart nearly robbed (빼앗다(of)) her of her breath. But on (계속해서) she flew toward the red entrance which led (이끌었다) to her people and her queen.

On the flying-board (판(꿀벌이 집에서 날아갈 준비를 하는 곳)), two sentinels blocked the entrance and laid hands upon her. Maya was too breathless to utter a syllable (한마디, 음절), and the sentinels threatened to kill her. For a bee to force its way into a strange city without the queen's consent is a **capital** (사형에 처해야 할, 중요한) **offense** (위반, 범죄).

"Stand back!" cried one sentinel, thrusting (밀치다) her roughly away. "What's the matter with you! If you don't leave this instant, you'll die.—Did you ever!" He turned to the other sentinel. "Have you ever seen the like, and before daytime too?"

Now Maya pronounced (발음하다) the password by which all the bees knew one another. The sentinels instantly released (놔주다, 풀어주다) her.

"What!" they cried. "You are one of us, and we don't know you?"

"Let me get to the queen," groaned the little bee.

"Right away, quick! We are in terrible danger."

The sentinels still hesitated. They couldn't **grasp**(파악하다) the situation(상황).

"The queen may not be awakened before sunrise," said the one.

"Then," Maya screamed, her voice rising to a passionate(격렬한) yell such as the sentinels had probably never heard from a bee before, "then the queen will never wake up alive. Death is following at my heels(뒤꿈치). Take me to the queen! Take me to the queen, I say!" Her voice was so wild and wrathful(격노한) that the sentinels were frightened, and obeyed(복종하다).

The three hurried together through the warm, well-known streets and corridors. Maya recognized everything, and for all her excitement and the tremendous need for haste, her heart quivered with sweet melancholy at the sight of the dear familiar(익숙한) scenes(현장).

"I am at home," she stammered with pale lips.

In the queen's reception(응접) room she almost broke down(무너졌다). One of the sentinels supported(부축하다, 지지하다) her while the other hurried with the unusual message into the private chambers(그 사적인 방(여왕의 방을 말함)). Both of them now realized that something **momentous**(중대한) was taking place, and the messenger ran as fast as his legs would carry him.

The first wax-generators(발생시키는 사람, 만드는 사람) were already up(일어난). Here and there a little head thrust itself out curiously from the openings. The news of the incident(사건) traveled quickly.

Two officers(장교) emerged from the private chambers. Maya recognized them instantly. In solemn(엄숙한) silence, without a word to her, they took their posts(근무 장소), one on each side of the doorway: the queen would soon appear.

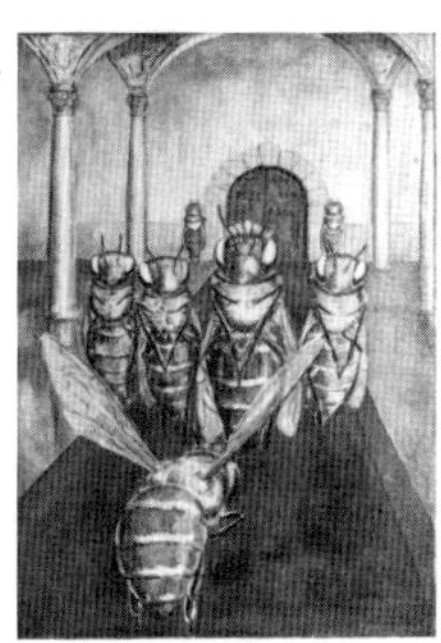

She came without her court(신하), attended(시중받다) only by her aide(보좌관) and two ladies-in-waiting(시녀(여왕을 모시는 귀족 부인)). She hurried straight over to Maya. When she saw what a state(상태) the child was in, the severe(심각한) expression on her face relaxed(누그러지다, 완화하다) a little.

"You have come with an important message? Who are you?"

Maya could not speak at once. Finally she managed to frame(입으로 말하다, 고안하다) two words:

"The hornets!"

The queen turned pale. But her **composure**(침착) was unshaken(흔들리지 않는), and Maya was somewhat calmed(차분해진).

"Almighty(절대의) queen!" she cried. "Forgive(용서하다) me for not respecting the duties I owe(빚지다) Your Majesty(폐하). Later I will tell you everything I have done. I **repent** (후회하다, 죄 등을 뉘우치다). With my whole heart I repent.—Just a little while ago, as by a miracle, I escaped from the fortress of the hornets, and the last I heard was that they were planning to attack and plunder (약탈하다) our kingdom at dawn."

The wild dismay (당황, 경악) that the little bee's words produced (생산하다) was indescribable (형언할 수 없는). The ladies-in-waiting set up (시작하다) a loud wail, the officers at the door turned pale and made as if to dash off and sound (소리를 울리다) the alarm (경고), the aide said: "Good God!" and wheeled completely round, because he wanted to see on all sides at once.

As for the queen, it was really extraordinary (비범한) to see with what composure, what resourcefulness (수완(어떤 일을 잘 처리함)) she received (받다) the dreadful news. She drew herself up, and there was something in her **attitude** (태도) that both **intimidate**d (위압하다, 두려워하게 하다) and inspired endless confidence (신뢰감). Little Maya was awed. Never, she felt, had she witnessed (목격하다) anything so superior (뛰어난). It was like a great, magnificent event (사건) in itself.

The queen beckoned the officers to her side and uttered a few rapid **sentence**s (문장, 말) aloud. At the end Maya heard:

"I give you one minute for the **execution** (집행, 실행) of my orders. A fraction (작은 부분) of a second longer, and it will cost (값을 치르게 하다) you your heads."

But the officers scarcely looked as if they needed this **incentive** (자극(늦으면 죽이겠다는)). In less time than it takes to tell they were gone. Their instant readiness was a joy to behold (보다).

"O my queen!" said Maya.

The queen inclined (기울이다) her head to the little bee, who once again for a brief moment saw her **monarch** (군주)'s **countenance** (용모) beam upon (~에게 방긋 웃다) her gently, lovingly.

"You have our thanks," she said. "You have saved us. No matter what your previous (전의) **conduct** (행위, 행동) may have been, you have made up for (보상했다) it a thousandfold (천배로).—But go, rest now, little girl, you look very miserable (몸이 좋지 않은, 비참한), and your hands are trembling."

"I should like to die for you," Maya stammered, quivering.

"Don't worry about us," replied the queen. "Among the thousands inhabiting (거주하다, 살다) this city there is not one who would hesitate a moment to sacrifice (희생시키다) his life for me and for the welfare (복지) of the country. You can go to sleep peacefully."

She bent over and kissed the little bee on her forehead. Then she beckoned to the ladies-in-waiting and bade (명령했다) them see to (~을 돌보다, ~을 준비하다) Maya's rest and comfort.

Maya, stirred (감동받았다) to the depths of her being (그녀의 깊은 곳(본심)까지), allowed (허락하다) herself to be led away. After this, life had nothing lovelier to offer (이것 뒤에 삶은 더 사랑스러운 것을 주지 않을 거다(이 순간이 가장 행복했다)). As in a dream she heard the loud, clear signals (신호) in the distance, saw the high dignitaries (dignitary 고관, 고위인사) of state assemble (모이다) around the royal chambers, heard a dull, far-echoing drone (윙윙거림) that shook the hive from roof to foundation (기초).

"The soldiers! Our soldiers!" whispered the ladies-in-waiting at her side.

The last thing Maya heard in the little room where her companions put her to bed was the tramp (무거운 발걸음 소리, 걷다) of soldiers marching past her door and commands shouted in a **blithe** (활기찬, 쾌활한), resolute (굳건한, 의지가 굳은), ringing (울려퍼지는) voice. Into her dreams, echoing as from a great distance, she carried (노래의 주 선율을 불렀다) the ancient song of the soldier-bees:

Sunlight, sunlight, golden sheen,
By your glow our lives are lighted;
Bless (축복하다) our labors, bless our Queen,
Let us always be united (합친, 단합한).

CHAPTER 16

THE BATTLE

The kingdom of the bees was in a whirl (소용돌이) of excitement. Not even in the days of the revolution (혁명) had the **turmoil** (동요, 혼란) been so great. The hive rumbled (우르르 울리다) and roared. Every bee was fired (흥분되다, 감정이 불타오르다) by a holy wrath, a burning **ardor** (열정) to meet and fight the ancient enemy to the very last gasp (숨이 멎음, 숨참). Yet there was no disorder (무질서) or confusion (혼란). Marvelous (놀라운) the speed with which the regiments (연대, 무리) were mobilized (동원되다), marvelous the way each soldier knew his duty and fell into his right place and took up (시작했다) his right work.

It was high time (한창때, 무르익은 때). At the queen's call for volunteers (지원자) to defend (방어하다) the entrance, a number of (많은) bees offered themselves, and of these several had been sent out to see if the enemy was approaching. Two had now returned—whizzing dots—and reported that the hornets were drawing near.

An awesome hush of **expectancy** fell upon the hive. Soldiers in three closed ranks stood lined up at the entrance, proud, pale, solemn, composed. No one spoke. The silence of death **prevail**ed, except for the low commands of the officers drawing up the **reserve**s in the **rear**. The hive seemed to be fast asleep. The only stir came from the doorway where about a dozen wax-generators were at work in **feverish** silence executing their orders to narrow the entrance with wax. As by a miracle, two thick partitions of wax had already gone up, which even the strongest hornets could not **batter** down without great loss of time. The hole had been **reduce**d by almost half.

The queen took up an elevated position inside the hive from which she was able to survey the battle. Her aides flew **scurry**ing hither and thither.

The third messenger returned. He sank down exhausted at the queen's feet.

"I am the last who will return," he shouted with all the strength he had left. "The others have been killed."

"Where are the hornets?" asked the queen.

"At the lindens!—Listen, listen," he stammered in mortal(지독한, 죽음의) terror, "the air hums with the wings of the giants."

No sound was heard. It must have been the poor fellow's terrified(끔찍한) imagination(상상), he must have thought he was still being pursued(쫓기는 중인).

"How many are there?" asked the queen sternly(엄하게). "Answer in a low voice."

"I counted forty."

Although the queen was startled by the enemy's numbers, she gave no sign of shock.

In a ringing, confident(자신감 있는) voice that all could hear, she said:

"Not one of them will see his home again."

Her words, which seemed to sound the enemy's doom(죽을 운명), had instant(즉각적인) effect. Men and officers alike(한결같이) felt their courage rise.

But when in the quiet of the morning an **ominous**(불길한, 불온한) whirring was heard outside the hive, first softly, then louder and louder, and the entrance darkened(어두워지다), and the whispering voices of the hornets, the most frightful(무시무시한) robbers and **murderers**(살인자) in the insect world, **penetrated**(침투하다) into the hive, then the faces of the **valiant**(용맹한) little bees turned pale as if washed over by a drab(담갈색) light falling upon their ranks. They gazed at one another with eyes in which death sat waiting, and those who were **ranged**(배치하다, 정렬시키다) at the entrance knew full well that one moment more and all would be over with them.

The queen's controlled(억제된) voice came clear and tranquil from her place on high:

"Let the robbers enter one by one until I give orders to attack(공격하다). Then those at the front throw themselves upon the **invaders**(침입자) a hundred at a time(한번에), and the ranks(열) behind cover(가리다) the entrance. In that way we shall divide up the enemy's forces(군대). Remember, you at the front, upon your strength and **endurance**(인내) and bravery(용맹) depends(의지하다(upon(on))) the fate of the whole state. Have no fear; in the dusk(어스름) the enemy will not see right away how well prepared we are, and he will enter unsuspecting(의심하지 않은 채)..."

She broke off. There, thrust through the doorway, was the head of the first brigand. The feelers played about, groping(grope더듬다), cautious, the pincers(집게이빨, 집게발) opened and closed. It was a blood-curdling(굳게 하는(curdle 굳게 하다)) sight. Slowly the huge black-and-gold striped(줄무늬의) body with its strong wings crept in after the head. The light falling in from the outside (바깥에서부터 안으로 떨어지는 빛) drew gleams (번쩍임) from the warrior's cuirass (허리 갑옷).

Something like a quiver went through the ranks of the bees, but the silence remained unbroken.

The hornet withdrew (물러났다) quietly. Outside he could be heard announcing (announce 발표하다):

"They're fast asleep. But the entrance is half walled (벽을 쌓다) up and there are no sentinels. I do not know whether to take this as a good or a bad sign."

"A good sign!" rang out. "Forward!"

At that two giants leapt in through the entrance side by side; after them, soundlessly (소리없이), pressed (밀고 나아가다) a **throng** (다수, 군중) of striped, armed, gleaming warriors, awful to behold. Eight made their way into the hive. Still no orders to attack from the queen. Was she dumb (벙어리의) with horror, had her voice failed her?

And the brigands, did they not see in the shadow, to right and left, the soldiers drawn up (정렬해 있는) in close, glittering ranks ready for mortal combat (전투)...?

Now at last came the order from on high:

"In the name of eternal (영원한) right (정의), in the name of your queen, to the defense of the realm (왕국, 영토)!"

At that a droning roar went up. Never before had

the city been shaken by such a battle-cry. It threatened(위협하다) to burst the hive in two. Where, an instant before, the hornets had been visible singly(하나씩), there were now buzzing heaps(덩어리), thick, dark, rolling knots. A young officer had scarcely awaited the end of the queen's words. He wanted to be the first to attack. He was the first to die. He had stood for some time ready to leap all a-quiver with eagerness for battle, and at the first sound of the order he rushed forward right into the clutches(수중) of the foremost brigand. His delicately fine-pointed(미세한 끝의) sting found its way between the head and upper breast-ring of his opponent; he heard the hornet give a yell of rage, saw him double up(몸을 구부리다) into a glittering, gold-black ball. Then the bandit's fearful sting leapt out and pierced between the young officer's breast-rings right into his heart; and dying the bee felt himself and his mortally(죽을 정도로) wounded(부상당한) enemy sink under a cloud of storming(맹공을 가하다) bees. His brave death inspired them all with the wild rapture that comes from utter willingness(기꺼이 함) to die for a noble(고귀한) cause(대의, 대의명분). Fearful was their attack upon the invaders. The hornets were sore(아픈, 지독한) pressed(압박 받았다).

But the hornets are an old race of robbers, trained(훈련 받았다) to warfare(전쟁). **Pillage**(약탈) and murder(살인) have long been their gruesome(소름끼치는) profession(직업). Though the initial(처음의) assault of the bees had confused and divided them, yet the damage(해, 손상) was not so great as might have seemed at first. For the bees' stings did not penetrate their breastplates((갑옷의) 가슴받이), and their strength and gigantic size gave them an advantage(장점) of which they were well aware(아는). Their sharp, buzzing battle-cry rose high above the battle-cry of the bees. It is a sound that fills all creatures with horror, even human beings, who dread this danger signal, and are careful not to enter into **conflict**(다툼, 싸움) with hornets unprotected(무방비의).

Those of the **assailant**(공격자)s who had already penetrated into the hive quickly realized that they must make their way still deeper inward if they were not to block up the entrance to their **comrade**(동료)s outside. And so the struggling knots(무리, 일단, 혹) rolled farther and farther down the dark streets and corridors. How right the queen had been in her **tactics**(전술)! No sooner(~하자마자 than~하다) was a bit of space at the entrance cleared(치워졌다) than the ranks in the rear leapt forward to its defense. It was an old **strategy**(전략), and a dreadful one for the enemy. When a hornet at the entrance gave signs of exhaustion(지침), the bees **sham**(가장하다, ~인 체하다)med the same, and let him crawl in; but the instant the one behind showed his head a great swarm(떼, 무리) of fresh soldiers dashed up to defend the apparently(보기에) unprotected(무방비의) entrance, while the invader who had gone on ahead would find himself, already wearied(지친), suddenly **confront**(마주하다, 대결하다)ed by glittering ranks of soldier-bees who had not yet stirred a finger in battle. Generally he **succumb**(지다, 굴복하다)ed to their superior numbers at the very first attack.

Now the groans(신음) of the wounded and the shrieks of the dying mingled(섞인) in wild agony(고통) with the fierce battle-cries. The hornets' stings worked fearful **havoc**(대혼란) among the bees. The rolling knots left tracks(길) of dead bodies in their **wake**(지나간 자국). The hornets, whose retreat(후퇴) had been cut off(차단 되었다), realizing that they would never see the light of day again, fought the fight of despair. Yet, slowly, one by one, they succumbed. There was one great thing against them. Though their strength was **inexhaustible**(지칠 줄 모르는), not so the poison(독) of their sting. After a time their sting lost its **virulence**(독성), and the wounded bees, knowing they'd recover(회복하다), fought in the consciousness(의식, 자각) of certain victory. To this was added(더해졌다) the grief(슬픔) of the bees for their dead; it gave them the power of divine(인간을 초월한, 신이 주신) wrath.

Gradually the **din**(소음) **subside**(가라앉다, 진정되다)d. The loud calls of the hornets on the outside met with no response from the invaders within.

"They are all dead," said the leader of the hornets grimly(섬뜩하게, 잔인하게), and summoned(호출하다) the combatants(전투원) back from the entrance. Their numbers had melted down(차차 없어지다) to half.

"We have been betrayed(비밀이 누설되었다)," said the leader. "The bees were prepared."

The hornets were assembled on the silver-fir(전나무). It had grown lighter, and the red of dawn **tinge**d(엷은 빛깔로 물들이다) the tops of the linden-trees. The birds began to sing. The dew fell. Pale and quivering with rage of battle, the warriors stood around their leader, who was waging(wage (수)행하다) an awful inward struggle. Should he **yield**(내주다) to **prudence**(현명함, 신중) or to his lust(욕망, 정욕) for pillage(약탈)? The former(먼저의 것) prevailed(우세하다). There was no use anyway. His whole tribe was in danger of destruction(파괴). **Grudgingly**(마지못해), in a **shudder**(떨림) of **thwart**ed(훼방놓다, 좌절시키다) ambition(야망), he determined to send a messenger to the bees to sue(청원하다) for the return of the prisoners.

He chose his cleverest officer and called upon him by name.

A depressed silence instead of an answer. The officer was among those who had been cut off(차단된, 갇힌).

The leader, overcome(압도당해) now by mortal(지독한) dread lest(~하지 않을까) those who had entered would never return, quickly chose another officer. The raging(사납게 날뛰는 소리) and roaring in the beehive could be heard in the distance.

"Be quick!" he cried, laying(두다, 놓다) the white petal of a jasmine in the messenger's hand, "or the human beings will soon come and we shall be lost. Tell the bees we will go away and leave them in peace forever if they will deliver(넘겨주다, 전하다) up the prisoners."

The messenger rushed off. At the entrance he waved his white signal and alighted(내리다) on the flying-board.

The queen-bee was immediately informed(알리다) that an **emissary**(사절) was outside who wanted to make terms(협상, 조건), and she sent her aide(부관) to **parley**(정전 회담을 하다) with him. When he returned with his report she sent back this reply:

"We will deliver up the dead if you want to take them away. There are no prisoners. All of your people who invaded(침입하다) our **territory**(영토) are dead. Your promise never to return we do not believe. You may come again, whenever you wish. You will fare(대접을 받다) no better than you did today. And if you want to go on with the battle we are ready to fight to the last bee."

The leader of the hornets turned pale when this message was delivered to him. He clenched(꽉 쥐다) his fists(주먹), he fought with himself. Only too gladly would he have yielded to the wishes of his warriors who **clamor**ed for (~해달라고 시끄럽게 요구하다(for), 함성) **revenge** (복수). Reason (이성) prevailed.

"We will come again," he hissed. "How could this thing have happened to us? Are we not a more powerful people than the bees? Every **campaign** (군사 작전, 전투) of mine so far has been successful (성공한) and has only added to our glory. How can I face the queen after this defeat (패배)?" In a quiver of fury he cried again: "How could this thing have happened to us? There must be **treachery** (배신, 배신행위) somewhere."

An older hornet known as a friend of the queen's here took up the word.

"It is true, we are a more powerful race, but the bees are a unified (단결된) nation, and unflinchingly (움츠리지 않게(flinch 움찔하다)) loyal to their people and their state. That is a great source (원천) of strength; it makes them **irresistible** (저항할 수 없는). Not one of them would turn **traitor** (배신자, 반역자); each without thought of self serves the weal (안녕, 복지) of all."

The leader scarcely listened.

"My day is coming," he hissed. "What care I for the wisdom (지혜) of these bourgeois (중산계급, 부르주아)! I am a brigand and will die a brigand.—But to keep up the battle now would be madness (미친 짓). What good would it do us if we destroyed the whole hive, and none of us came back alive?" Turning to the messenger, he cried:

"Give us back our dead. We will withdraw(철수하다)."

A dead silence fell. The messenger flew off.

"We must be prepared for a fresh piece of **trickery**(속임수, 계략), though I don't think the hornets are in a fighting mood at present(현재에)," said the queen bee when she heard the hornets' decision(결심). She gave orders for the rear-guard, wax-generators, and honey-carriers(운반하는 사람(꿀벌)) to remove(옮기다, 치우다) the dead from the city while two fresh regiments guarded the entrance.

Her orders were carried out(carry out 행하다, 수행하다). Over mountains of the dead one brigand's body after another was dragged(끌다) to the entrance and thrown to the ground outside.

In gloomy(우울한) silence the troop(군대) of hornets waited on the silver-fir and saw the **corpse**s(시체) of their fallen warriors drop one by one to the earth.

The sun arose upon a scene of endless desolation(황폐). Twenty-one slain(살해된 / slay(죽이다)의 과거분사), who had died a glorious death, made a heap in the grass under the city of the bees. Not a drop of honey, not a single prisoner had been taken by the enemy. The hornets picked up their dead and flew away, the battle was over, the bees had **conquer**ed(무찌르다, 이기다).

But at what a cost [희생]! Everywhere lay fallen bodies, in the streets and corridors, in the dim places before the brooders [부화장소(brood 알을 품다)] and honey-cupboards. Sad was the work in the hive on that lovely morning of summer sunshine and scented [향기나는] blossoms. The dead had to be **dispose**d of [처분하다, 치우다(of)], the wounded had to be bandaged [붕대를 감다] and nursed [간호하다]. But before the hour of noon had struck, the regular tasks [일] were begun; for the bees neither celebrated [축하하다] their victory nor spent time **mourn**ing [슬퍼하다] their dead. Each bee carried his pride and his grief locked [가둔, 간직한] quietly in his breast and went about his work.

CHAPTER 17

THE QUEEN'S FRIEND

The noise of battle awoke Maya out of a brief (짧은) sleep. She jumped up and straightway wanted to dash out to help defend the city, but soon realized that she was too weak to be of any help.

A group of struggling combatants (전투원) came rolling toward her. One of them was a strong young hornet, an officer, Maya judged by his badge (배지), who was defending himself unaided (도움을 받지 않고) against an overwhelming (압도적인) number of bees. The struggling knot (무리) drew nearer. To Maya's horror it left one dead bee after another in its wake. But numbers finally told against (불리하게 작용했다(against) / tell 작용하다) (벌이 많아 그 거인(말벌)이 불리했다) the giant: whole clusters (무리, 떼) of bees, ready to die rather than let go, hung to his arms and legs and feelers, and their stings were beginning to pierce (뚫다) between the rings of his breast. Maya saw him drop down exhausted. Without cry or **complaint** (불평), fighting to the very end, neither suing for (sue for 청하다) mercy nor reviling (revile 욕하다) his opponents, he went down to his brigand's death.

The bees left him and hurried back to the entrance to throw themselves anew into the conflict (전쟁, 갈등).

Maya's heart was beating stormily. She slipped over to the hornet. He lay curled up in the twilight, still breathing. She counted about twenty stings, most of them in the fore part of his body, leaving his golden armor quite whole and sound (손상되지 않은). Seeing he was still alive, she hurried away to bring water and honey—to cheer the dying man, she thought. But he shook his head and waived her off with his hand.

"I take what I want," he said proudly. "I don't care for gifts."

"Oh," said Maya, "I only thought you might be thirsty."

The young officer smiled at her, then said, not sadly, but with a strange earnestness (진정함):

"I must die."

The little bee could not reply. For the first time in

her life she seemed to **comprehend**(이해하다) what it meant to have to die; and death seemed much closer when some-one else was about to die than when her own life had been **imperil**(위태롭게 하다)ed in the spider's web.

"If there were only something I could do," she said, and burst into tears.

The dying hornet made no answer. He opened his eyes once again and heaved a deep breath—for the last time. Half an hour later he was thrown down into the grass outside the hive along with his dead comrades.

Little Maya never forgot what she had learned from this brief farewell(작별). She knew now for all time that her enemies were beings like herself, loving life as she did and having to die a hard death without **succor**(구조, 원조). She thought of the flower sprite who had told her of his rebirth(재생) when Nature sent forth her blossoms again in the spring; and she longed to know whether the other crea-tures would, like the sprite, come back to the light of life after they had died the death of the earth.

"I will believe it is so," she said softly.

A messenger now came and summoned her to the queen's presence(면전). She found the full court assembled in the royal reception room. Her legs shook, she scarcely dared to raise her eyes before her monarch (군주) and so many dignitaries (고관들). A number of the officers of the queen's **staff** (보좌역, 자문단) were missing, and the gathering was unusually solemn. Yet a gleam of exaltation (의기양양) seemed to light every brow—as if the consciousness (자각) of triumph (승리) and new glory won (승리한, 얻은) encircled (둘러싸다) everyone like an invisible **halo** (후광(성인의 머리 둘레에 있는 빛)).

The queen arose, made her way unattended (시중을 받지 않은 채) through the **assemblage** (모임, 모인 사람들), went up to little Maya and took her in her arms.

This Maya had never expected, not this. The measure of her joy was full to overflowing (흘러넘치다); she broke down and wept.

The bees were deeply stirred. There was not one among them who did not share Maya's happiness, who was not deeply grateful (감사하는) for the little bee's valiant (용감한) deed (행위).

Maya now had to tell her whole story. Everybody wanted to know how she had learned of the hornets' plans and how she had succeeded in (성공하다(in)) breaking out of the awful prison from which no bee had ever before escaped.

So Maya told of all the remarkable things she had seen and heard, of Miss Loveydear with the glittering wings, of the grasshopper, of Thekla the spider, of Puck, and of how splendidly Bobbie had come to her rescue. When she told of the sprite and the human beings, it was so quiet in the hall that you could hear the generators ((밀랍을) 만드는 사람들(벌들)) in the back of the hive **knead**ing (반죽하다, 쉬어 이기다) the wax.

"Ah," said the queen, "who'd have thought the sprites were so lovely?" She smiled to herself with a look of melancholy and longing, as people will who long for beauty.

And all the dignitaries smiled the same smile.

"How did the song of the sprite go?" she asked. "Say it again. I'd like to learn it by heart."

Maya repeated the song of the sprite.

My soul is that which breathes anew
From all of loveliness and grace (우아함);
And as it flows from God's own face,
It flows from his creations (창조물들), too.

There was silence for a while. The only sound was a restrained (억제된) sobbing in the back of the hall—probably someone thinking of a friend who had been killed.

Maya went on with her story. When she came to the hornets, the bees' eyes darkened and widened. Each imagined himself in the situation in which one of their number had been, and quivered, and drew a deep breath.

"Awful," said the queen, "perfectly awful..."

The dignitaries murmured something to the same effect.

"And so," Maya ended, "I reached home. And I sue for your Majesty's pardon—a thousand times."

Oh, no one bore (가졌다) the little bee any ill will for having run away from the hive. You may imagine they did not.

The queen put her arm round Maya's neck.

"You did not forget your home and your people," she said kindly. "In your heart you were loyal. So we will be loyal to you. Henceforth (지금부터) you shall stay by my side and help me conduct the affairs of state. In that way, I think, your experiences, all the things you have learned, will be made to serve the greatest good of your people and your country."

Cheers of approval (시인, 찬성) greeted the queen's words.

So ends the story of the adventures of Maya the bee. They say her work **contribute**d (기여하다) greatly to the good and welfare of the nation, and she came to be highly respected (존경받는) and loved by her people. Sometimes on quiet evenings she went for a brief hour's conversation to

Cassandra's peaceful little room, where the ancient(나이 든) dame(부인) lived now on pension(연금) honey. There Maya told the young bees, who listened to her eagerly, stories of the adventures which we have lived through with her.

Essential Vocabulary

abide by	규칙 등에 따라 행동하다, 준수하다 adhere to; comply with, follow, observe
abuse	남용하다 to use wrongly or improperly; misuse
acquaintance	앎, 사귐 knowledge, experience
acrobatics	곡예 a kind of physical exercises, performing art
adage	격언 saying; proverb
agog	~로 흥분한, ~하고 싶어 못 견디는 excited, eager to
agony	괴로움, 고통 great physical, mental pain ; suffering
angular	모난, 각진 shapes with a lot of straight lines and sharp points
animate	활발하게 하다, 생명을 주다 make it lively or more cheerful; enliven
anticipation	기대 expectation ; a feeling of exciting that you know is going to happen
apply	사용하다, 활용하다 use; employ
apprehension	염려, 걱정 anxiety; concern; alarm
approval	승인, 시인 permission; sanction; consent
apt	~하기 쉬운 inclined; disposed; given; prone

arbitrary	제멋대로의, 임의의 not based on any principle, plan, or system. random; whimsical; capricious; impulsive
arbor	나무그늘의 휴식장소, 정자 a shelter in a garden which is formed by leaves and stems of plants
ardor	열정 enthusiasm; eagerness; avidity
aristocratic	귀족의 upper-class; blue-blooded; privileged
arrogance	거만, 오만 exaggerated self-opinion; aloofness; conceit;
artificial	인공의 made by human skill; produced by humans
artistic	예술적인 beautiful, satisfying to senses; aesthetic
assail	공격하다 to attack vigorously or violently; assault
assailant	공격자 a person who attacks; attacker; aggressor
assemblage	모임, 모인 사람들 a group of persons gathered or collected; an assembly; collection; aggregate.
assemble	모이다, 집합하다 to come together; gather; meet
assistance	도움 help; aid; support
associate	사귀다, 제휴하다 to join as a companion, partner, or ally
association	교제, 조합 friendship; companionship
atone	보상하다, 벌충하다 to make up, as for errors or deficiencies
attitude	태도 manner, disposition, feeling, position, etc

avidly	열광적으로 enthusiastic; ardent; dedicated
baleful	해로운, 악의가 있는 harmful, malign
banish	추방하다 exile; expatriate; outlaw; deport
barbed	가시가 있는 having barbs (cf. barb: a pointed part projecting backward from a main point)
batter	때려 부수다, 강타하다 to damage by beating or hard usage
be vanquished	패배하다, cf. vanquish 무찌르다, 패배시키다 beat; conquer; crush
bent	향한, 결심한 determined; set; resolved
bestow	주다 to present as a gift; give; confer
betray	누설하다, 배신하다 divulge; expose information; be disloyal
blank	멍한, 백지인 showing no attention, interest, or emotion; white
blithe	활기찬, 쾌활한 happy, mirthful, sprightly, light-hearted
blush	얼굴을 붉히다 to redden, as from embarrassment or shame
boast	자랑스럽게 말하다 to speak with pride; brag
booty	노획물, 약탈물 spoil taken from an enemy in war; plunder; pillage
border	경계선을 이루다, 이웃하다, 가깝다 to form a border to; adjoin
brittle	부서지기 쉬운 easily damaged or destroyed; fragile; frail

butt	머리로 받다 to strike or push with the head or horns
calamity	재난, 불운 disaster; a great misfortune
campaign	군사작전, 전투 military operations; battle
capital	사형에 처해야 할 punishable by death
carcass	시체 dead body; cadaver; corpse
catastrophe	재앙 a sudden and widespread disaster; misfortune, calamity
cavity	구멍, 공동 any hollow place; hollow
chagrin	분함 a feeling of vexation; shame; embarrassment, mortification
chrysalis	고치, 번데기 a pupa enclosed in a firm case or cocoon
clamber	기어오르다 to climb, using both feet and hands
clamor	~해달라고 시끄럽게 요구하다(for) cry out; make commotion
cling	~에 붙다 to adhere closely; stick to
clot	(덩어리로) 엉기다, 응고하다 to form into clots; coagulate (n. clot : a semisolid mass)
clumsy	서투른 unhandy, unskillful, maladroit, inexpert
clutch	손아귀, 붙잡음 the hand, claw; a tight grip or hold
collect	자제심을 되찾다, 모으다 to regain control of; to gather together; assemble
command	내려다보다 look down upon or over a body of water, region, etc

community	공동체 a social group of any size whose members reside in a specific locality
compare	비교하다, 견주다 to examine similarities and differences
comparison	비교 the act of comparing
compel	억지로 만들다, 강요하다 to force to do something; oblige; coerce
compensation	보상 recompense, payment, amends, reparation
complain	불평하다 grumble; growl; whine
complaint	불평 an expression of discontent, regret, pain
compliment	찬사, 아첨 praise; flatter
complimentary	무료의, 칭찬하는 given free ; expressing a compliment
composure	침착 self-controlled state of mind; calmness; tranquillity
comprehend	이해하다 understand; grasp with the mind; perceive
comrade	동료 companion; associate; friend
conceal	숨기다 to hide; cover or keep from sight
concealment	숨음, 은닉 the act of hiding; the state of being concealed
conceive	품다 to hold as an opinion; think; believe
conception	개념, 생각 a notion; idea; concept

conduct	행위, 행동 personal behavior; way of acting
confidence	확신, 자신 certitude; assurance
conflict	다툼, 싸움 fight; battle; struggle
conform	규칙 등에 따르다 to act in accordance or harmony; comply
congeal	굳어지다 harden, set, jell, solidify
conquer	무찌르다, 이기다 to overcome by force; subdue
conscious	자각하는, 알아차린 knowing; percipient; aware
consequence	결과 effect; result; outcome
consist of	~로 구성되어 있다 to be made up or composed
constrained	강요당한(constrain 강요하다, 억압하다) forced; compelled; obliged
contemplatively	골똘히, 명상하는 듯한 thoughtfully; reflectively; meditatively
contempt	경멸 disdain; scorn
contradict	반박하다, 이의를 제기하다 gainsay, impugn, controvert, dispute
contradictory	상반되는, 모순되는 contradicting; inconsistent; logically opposite
contribute	기여하다 to be an important factor in; help to cause
contrivance	고안품 something contrived; a device
corpse	시체 a dead body; cadaver

corpulent	뚱뚱한 large or bulky of body; portly; stout; fat
corridor	복도(나무에 판 구멍을 말함)
count	중요하다 to have importance, value
countenance	행위, 행동 behavior
cove	작은 만, 후미진 곳 a small indentation in the shoreline of a sea
cower	움츠리다 to crouch in fear
crevice	갈라진 틈 a crack; cleft; rift; fissure
cripple	부자유스럽게 하다, 불구를 만들다 to disable; impair; weaken
criticize	비평하다 to make judgments as to merits and faults
cull	꽃을 따 모으다, 추려내다 to pick out and put aside as inferior
curtail	줄이다, 단축하다 to cut short; ; abridge; reduce; diminish
damage	손상하다, 해치다 injure; harm
dauntless	두려움을 모르는, 불굴의 fearless; intrepid; bold
dazzle	눈부심 shining or reflecting brilliantly
decay	썩는 to become decomposed; rot
decline	거절하다 to refuse with courtesy
deliberation	협의, 토의, 신중함 formal discussion; reflection; forethought

denunciation	비난, 탄핵 an accusation; public censure or condemnation
deserted	사람이 없는 untenanted: without inhabitants
desertion	도망, 탈주, 버림 an act of leaving duty; willful abandonment
detect	간파하다, 탐지하다 to discover some actions or the existence
determination	결의 firmness of purpose; the settlement of a dispute, question
devolve	옮겨지다, 맡겨지다 to transfer or delegate
devote	바치다, 전념하다 to concentrate on a particular pursuit; dedicate
devour	게걸스레 먹다 to swallow or eat up hungrily
diagonal	대각선의 having an oblique direction
din	소음 a loud, confused noise
disarm	마음을 누그러뜨리게 하다, 무장을 해제하다 to relieve of hostility; to lay down one's weapons
dislocate	관절 등이 빠지다, 위치를 바꾸다 to put out of joint or out of position
dismember	팔다리를 잘라버리다 to deprive of limbs
dispose	처분하다, 치우다(of) to get rid of; discard
distinguish	유명하게 하다, 구별하다 to make prominent, conspicuous; differentiate
distract	주의를 딴 데로 돌리다 to draw away the attention
divine	추측하다, 예언하다, 신의 to conjecture; prophesy; godlike

dominate	지배하다, 복종하다 govern; predominate
doom	운명, 비운, 파멸 fate or destiny; ruin; death
dorsal	등의 pertaining to the back
drape	싸다, 걸치다 to cover or hang with cloth
droop	눈을 내리깔다, 머리 등을 숙이다
dub	기사 작위를 주다 designate as a knight
duck	고개 숙이다 to stoop or bend suddenly
dusk	어스름, 해질녘 the dark part of twilight
dwelling	주택, 주거 place of residence; abode
emanate	나오다, 퍼지다 to flow out; to issue
embitter	적개심을 품게 하다 envenom; cause to feel bitterness
emissary	사절 delegate; ambassador; envoy
emphatic	강조된, 강경한 using emphasis; forceful; insistent
enchantment	마법을 걸기 the act of enchanting
endurable	견딜 수 있는 bearable; tolerable
endurance	인내 patience; bearing pain, hardships
enmesh	말려들다, 그물에 걸리다 entangle; to catch in a net

entangle	얽히게 하다 ensnarl; intertwine
enthrone	왕좌에 앉다 To seat on a throne
entrench	침범하다, 참호를 파다 to encroach; trespass; infringe; to dig trenches
entrust	맡기다 to commit (something) in trust to; confide
enviable	부러운, 샘나는 worthy of envy; very desirable
equip	필요한 것을 갖추다 to furnish; to prepare
eternal	영원한 lasting forever; perpetual
exception	예외 the act of excepting; exclusion
execution	집행, 실행 the act or process of executing
expand	팽창하다 extend; swell; enlarge
expectancy	기대, 예상 expectation; anticipatory belief or desire
exposed	(위험 등에) 노출된 susceptible to attack; vulnerable
exquisite	아주 아름다운 dainty; beautiful; elegant
extinguish	불 등을 끄다 quench; smother; snuff out; blow out
exult	기뻐 날뛰다 delight; glory; revel
fang	송곳니 one of the long, sharp, hollow or grooved teeth
feebler	약한, 희미한 feeble: lacking strength; weak

feeler	더듬이 an organ of touch, as an antenna
feverish	들뜬, 초조한 excited; restless; uncontrolled
filter	투과시키다 to pass or slip through slowly
flare	타오름, 감정 등의 격발 erupt; explode; flash; blaze; flame
flinch	움찔하다 recoil; withdraw; blench
flourish	팔 등을 휘두르다 to make dramatic, sweeping gestures
flurried	혼란스러운 marked by confusion or agitation
fluster	당황하게 하다 upset; bewilder; disconcert; disturb
flutter	두근거림, 흥분, 날개짓 a state of nervous excitement;
foliage	전체 잎 the leaves of a plant, collectively
formidable	무서운, 위협적인 dreadful, appalling, threatening, menacing
fraction	부분 portion; section
fragrant	향기로운 having a pleasant scent; sweet-smelling
frame	마음에 품다, ~을 떠올리다, ~을 짜맞추다 to conceive or imagine, as an idea
freebooter	약탈자, 해적 pirate; buccaneer
frivolous	경망스러운 given to trifling or undue levity
fulfill	이루다, 성취하다 accomplish; achieve; complete

furnish	제공하다 to provide; to supply
furrow	고랑, 밭고랑 a narrow groovelike or trenchlike depression
furtive	은밀한 clandestine; covert
gad	나다니다 to move restlessly or aimlessly
genuine	진지한, 진짜의 sincere; origin; not counterfeit; authentic; real
give out	동나다, 바닥이 나다 to become used up
glee	환희 exultant joy; exultation
glossy	광택 있는 shining, polished, glazed
grain	낟알, 곡물, 곡식 a small, hard seed; the seed of a food plant
grasp	파악하다 comprehend; understand
grave	위험을 내포한, 장엄한 threatening a seriously bad outcome; solemn
grudgingly	마지못해 displaying or reflecting reluctance or unwillingness
guilty	죄의식의 having or showing a sense of guilt
halo	후광(성인의 머리 둘레에 있는 빛) a radiant light around or above the head of a divine or sacred personage
handicapped	신체적인 장애가 있는 physically disabled
hanker	갈망하다 to have a restless or incessant longing

harbor	마음속에 품다, 숨겨주다, 항구 to maintain; entertain; conceal; hide
havoc	대혼란 great destruction; devastation
hazard	위험 danger; peril; risk; difficulty
hide	가죽 the pelt or skin of the larger animals or a human being
host	다수, 많은 무리 swarm; crowd; drove; throng
humdrum	단조로운, 지루한 tedious; routine; mundane; tiresome
hurl	세게 던지다 cast; pitch
hush	조용함 silence; quiet
immaculate	얼룩하나 없이 깨끗한, 깨끗한 free from spot or stain; spotlessly clean
immemorial	먼 옛날의 timeless; ancient; ageless; olden
impel	억지로 ~하게 하다 to urge to action through moral pressure
imperil	위태롭게 하다 risk; jeopardize; hazard
impervious	영향을 받지 않는, 통과시키지 않는 incapable of being influenced; impenetrable
impractical	비실용적인, 비현실적인 impracticable; idealistic
impulse	충동 an impelling force; an impetus
incentive	자극 stimulus; spur; incitement
incident	사건 an individual occurrence or event; happening

inconspicuous	주의를 끌지 않는 unnoticeable; unobtrusive; unostentatious
indelicate	섬세하지 않은, 거친 not delicate; lacking delicacy; rough
indescribable	말로 표현할 수 없는 indefinable; unutterable
indulgently	너그럽게 characterized by or showing indulgence
inexhaustible	지칠 줄 모르는 untiring; tireless
infuriating	격노케 하는 causing to anger or outrage; maddening
inhabitant	거주자 dweller; denizen
inkling	암시, 넌지시 비침 hint; intimation
inquisitive	호기심어린, 연구를 좋아하는 eager for knowledge; intellectually curious
insert	삽입하다, 끼워 넣다 to put or place in
insinuate	넌지시 말하다 to suggest or hint slyly
insolence	오만, 거만, 무례 contemptuously rude; impertinent behavior
inspire	생기게 하다 to produce; to arouse
in store for	~을 위해 준비된(저장된) in readiness or reserve for
intent	의도 purpose; design; intention
interfere	방해하다, 간섭하다 obstruct; meddle
intimidate	위압하다, 두려워하게 하다 frighten; subdue; daunt; terrify

invader	침입자 someone who enter forcefully as an enemy
irresistible	저항할 수 없는 incapable of being withstood
irritation	안달, 짜증 anger; annoyance; discomfort
jog	기억을 불러일으키게 하다, 조깅하다 nudge; run
jostle	서로 밀치다 to bump; push; shove
justification	정당화 an explanation that justifies or defends
kidney	신장, 콩팥 a pair of bean-shaped organs in the back
knead	반죽하다, 섞어 이기다 to work into a uniform mixture by pressing
laconically	(말을) 간결하게 briefly; pithily; tersely
languish	낙담한, 기운이 없는 weak; feeble; droop; fade
larva	애벌레 the immature, wingless stage of an insect
lay down the law	거만한 태도로 명령하다 to assert firmly the law
like as not	아마, 십중팔구 in all probability
limber	유연하게 하다(up) to make something flexible
lineage	가계, 혈통 pedigree; parentage; derivation
literature	문학 writings expressing ideas of permanent and universal interest
luminous	빛나는 reflecting light; shining; bright

lurch	비틀거림, 갈짓자 걸음, 배 등의 갑작스런 기울 an awkward, swaying or staggering motion
lure	유혹하다 to attract; entice; tempt
lurk	잠복하다, 숨어 기다리고 있다 to lurk; skulk; sneak; prowl
lust	욕망, 정욕 a desire; craving
magnet	자석 a piece of iron or steel attracting certain substances
massacre	학살하다, 대학살 slay; carnage; extermination; butchery; genocide
meandering	굽이도는, 구불구불한 turning; winding
meditate	곰곰이 생각하다, 명상하다 ponder; muse; ruminate
minute	미세한 concerned with even the smallest details; detailed; exact
momentous	중대한 vital; critical; crucial; serious
monarch	군주 a hereditary sovereign
morsel	맛있는 음식, 음식물의 한 입 tidbit; a mouthful portion of food
mortal	지독한, 죽을 운명의 severe; dire; grievous; fatal
mortification	억울, 분함, 굴욕 humiliation; shame
mortify	굴욕감을 주다 humble; abase
mourn	슬퍼하다 bewail; bemoan
murder	죽이다 to kill; slaughter

murderer	살인자 a person who commits murder
nerve	정력, 활력, 신경 strength; vigor; energy
nourishment	음식물, 영양 food; nutriment
nuisance	귀찮은 존재 an obnoxious or annoying person, thing
nuptial	결혼식의, 결혼 pertaining to marriage; a wedding
objection	이의, 반대 disagreement; opposition; refusal; disapproval
observation	관측, 관찰(전망대) an act of regarding attentively or watching
odoriferous	악취를 풍기는, 향기 나는 malodorous; fragrant; aromatic; perfumed
offense	위반, 범죄 a transgression; a violation
ominous	불길한, 불온한 portentous; threatening; menacing; fateful
on her own hook	스스로의 책임으로, 혼자 힘으로 on one's own responsibility; independently
overwhelm	압도하다 to overpower; destroy; crush
pang	상심, 비통, 번민 distress ; twinge
paralyzing	마비시키는 bring to a condition of helpless stoppage
parley	정전회담을 하다 an informal conference between enemies under a truce
peculiarity	별남, 기발함 oddity; singularity; eccentricity
pelt	(비 등이) 내리치다, 두들기다 to beat or pound unrelentingly

penetrate	침투하다 to enter and diffuse itself through; permeate
pensive	생각에 잠긴, 애수 띤 thoughtful
peremptory	위압적인, 독단적인 imperious; dictatorial
perish	멸망하다 to suffer destruction or ruin
permeate	투과하다, 퍼지다 to pass into or through every part of
personality	성격, 인격 whole character and nature
pert	주제넘은, 건방진 presumptuous, impudent
pillage	약탈 rapine; depredation; spoliation
pincer	집게발, 집게 a hand tool for holding
placid	조용한 peaceful; unruffled; tranquil
plight	곤경, 궁지 predicament; dilemma
plump	포동포동한 portly; fleshy; stout; fat
plunder	약탈하다 to rob; despoil; fleece
pollen	꽃가루 the fertilizing element of flowering plants
porous	다공성의, 구멍이 많은 full of pores
portal	입구 a door; gate; entrance
possess	가지다 to have; hold; occupy; own

pounce	덮치다 to swoop down suddenly and grasp
predecessor	전임자 a person who precedes another in an office, position
preen	몸치장을 하다 to trim; dress
premise	전제 assumption; postulate
presume	추정하다 presuppose
prevail	지배적이다, 널리 퍼져 있다 predominate; to be widespread
previous	전의 earlier; former; preceding; foregoing
prime	가장 중요한 primary; of the first importance
proboscis	곤충의 주둥이, 입 beak; the elongate, protruding mouth parts of certain insects
proclaim	발표하다, 선언하다 to announce; declare
profit	도움이 되다 to be beneficial to
prop	괴다, 기대다 to support or sustain
property	재산, 자산 belongings
prosperity	번영 a successful, flourishing, or thriving condition
protuberant	돌출한 bulging out; protruding; projecting
prudence	현명함, 신중 caution; discretion
prudent	분별 있는 wise; judicious; sagacious

pry	떼내다, 엿보다 peer; peep
pungent	신랄한, 자극하는 sarcastic; mordant; cutting; stimulating
pupa	번데기 an insect in transformation stage between the larva and the imago
pursuit	추적 chase; hunt
quality	품질, 질 how good or bad it is
quit	떠나다, 떠나가다, 그만두다 to depart from; leave; stop
quiver	떨다 quake; shudder; shiver
radiance	빛남 resplendence; splendor; brilliance
radiant	빛나는 beaming; refulgent; resplendent
range	배치하다, 정렬시키다 to draw up or arrange; set in order
rank	순위를 차지하다 to take up or occupy a place
rapture	기쁨, 환희 bliss; beatitude; transport; exaltation
rave	극찬하다, 헛소리하다 to talk with enthusiasm; to utter as if in madness
realm	영역, 국토 a region; sphere; domain
rear	뒤 the back of something
rebel	반역자 insurrectionist; mutineer; traitor

rebellion	반란 organized, and armed resistance to one's government or ruler
reckless	무모한 headstrong; rash
recluse	은둔자 a person who lives in seclusion or apart from society
recollection	회상 the act recalling to mind
recuperate	회복하다, 재기하다 to recover; restore
reduce	줄이다 diminish; decrease; shorten
refrain	삼가다, 억제하다 to abstain
release	풀어주다 to free from anything that restrains
remnant	나머지, 남은 부분 a remaining; remainder; residue
repent	후회하다, 죄 등을 뉘우치다 to feel sorry, self-reproachful, or contrite
requisite	필수 something requisite
resentment	분개, 적의 the feeling of displeasure or indignation
reserve	예비병력, 저장 fraction of a military force held in readiness; stock
resolve	결심, 결의 a resolution; determination
resplendent	눈부신, 화려한 gleaming; splendid
restrain	제한하다 to limit; hamper
retirement	은거, 칩거, 은퇴 seclusion; withdrawal from business

revenge	복수 retaliation; vengeance
revert	되돌아 가다 to return to a former condition
rotundity	구 모양, 원형, 통통함 the condition of roundness or plumpness
rumple	(머리털 등을) 헝클어뜨리다, 구기다 to ruffle; tousle
sacrifice	희생 the person, or thing offered, surrendered or devoted
sally forth	출격하다 set out in a sudden, energetic manner
salvation	구출, 구원 the act of saving or protecting
saucy	건방진, 뻔뻔스러운 impertinent; insolent
scientific	과학의 of or pertaining to the sciences
scrape	긁어내다, 문지르다 to scratch; rub
scurry	날쌔게 움직이다 to go or move quickly
seal	봉하다, 막다 to block; close
sear	시든, 마른, 태워 그을리다 to dry up or wither; burn the surface of
sentence	문장, 말 A grammatical unit that is independent and has a subject
separate	별도의, 개개의 to sort, part, divide, or disperse
seren	고요한, 잔잔한 calm; peaceful; tranquil; unruffled
sham	가장하다, ~인 체하다 to assume; pretend

shed	벗기다 to cast off; let fall
sheen	광택 luster; brightness; radiance
shred	조각, 단편 a piece cut or torn off; a particle
shrewdly	약삭빠르게 astute; sharp
shroud	덮다, 덮어 가리다 to cover; hide from view
shudder	떨림 a convulsive movement of the body
singular	기묘한, 보기 드문 peculiar; unusual or strange
sip	한 모금, 홀짝 마시기 a small taste of a liquid
skeleton	골격 the bones of a human or an animal forming the framework
slaughter	죽이다, 살해하다 to kill; butcher
snub	냉대하다, 퇴짜놓다 to treat with disdain or contempt; check or reject
solemnity	엄숙함 earnestness; gravity; impressiveness
solidarity	단결 union; fellowship
solitude	고독 the state of being or living alone; seclusion:
spell	마법, 주문 charm; incantation
sphere	구(球), 둥근 물체 any rounded body; a globular mass
spurn	퇴짜놓다, 거절하다, 업신여기다 to reject with disdain; scorn

squabble	쓸데없는 싸움을 하다 to engage in a petty quarrel
squeeze	쑤셔 넣다 to thrust forcibly; force by pressure; cram
staff	보좌역, 자문단 a group of assistants
stalk	줄기 the stem or main axis of a plant
statue	동상 A three-dimensional form sculpted, carved, or cast in material
steep	담그다, 적시다 to soak in a liquid
stench	악취 an offensive smell or odor; stink
still	가라앉히다 to calm, appease, or allay
stilt	죽마 one of two poles, each with a support for the foot
stir	감동시키다, 선동하다 to incite; instigate; or prompt
stout	뚱뚱한 thick; heavy
strain	최대한 일하다, 극도로 사용하다 to exert to the utmost
strategy	전략 a plan, method for obtaining a specific goal
stray	길에서 벗어나다 to digress
streak	줄 a long, narrow mark
strenuously	정력적으로, 활발히 vigorous; energetic; zealously active
strewn	흩뿌려진 to be scattered or sprinkled over

stripe	줄무늬 a relatively long, narrow band of a different color
strum	가볍게 치다, 퉁기다 to run the fingers lightly across the strings
stuck to	끝까지 지켰다, 충실했다 to remain firm; hold faithfully a promise
stump	그루터기, 밑둥 the lower end of a tree
subdued	완화된, 억제된 lowered in intensity; repressed
sublime	숭고한, 장엄한 inspiring awe, veneration:
subside	가라앉다, 진정되다 to become quiet; abate:
subsistence	존재, 생존 the state of existing
succession	연속, 계속 the coming of one person or thing after another in order
succor	구조, 원조 help; relief; aid; assistance
succumb	지다, 굴복하다 submit; accede; surrender
sue	청원하다, 고소하다 beg; petition; plead; pray
suggestion	제안 counsel; recommendation; suggestion; persuasion
suit	어울리다 to be appropriate or becoming to
sultry	무더운, 찌는 듯이 더운 oppressively hot; emitting great heat
summon	불러일으키다, 호출하다 to call into action; rouse; call forth
superior	으쓱하는, 거만한, 상위의 haughty; arrogant; snobbish

surly	퉁명스러운 churlishly rude; bad-tempered
survey	바라보다, 조사하다 to view in detail; to conduct a survey
suspension	매달기, 공중에 떠있기 the condition of being suspended or being hung
swarm	벌 등이 떼지어 움직이다 to move about, along in great numbers
swell	넘치다, 부풀다 to grow in bulk; inflate; expand
swerve	빗나가다 to turn aside
swoop	급강하하다 to come down upon something in a sudden
sympathize	동정하다 to feel a compassionate sympathy
sympathy	동정 fellow feeling, compassion, or commiseration
tackle	착수하다 to undertake to handle, master, solve
tactics	전술 any mode of procedure for gaining success
tangle	엉키게 하다 to bring together into a mass
taunt	비웃음, 비꼼 insulting; jeering manner; mock
terrestrial	육지의 of or pertaining to land
territory	영토 any tract of land; region; district
throb	고동치다 to pulsate; vibrate
throng	다수, 군중 crowd; horde; host; assemblage

thwart	훼방놓다, 좌절시키다 hinder; obstruct; frustrate
tide	조류, 밀물 the inflow, outflow, or current of water
timidity	소심한 easily alarmed; timorous; shy
tinge	엷은 빛깔로 물들이다 to tint
to say nothing	~은 말할 것도 없이 and also; not forgetting
toilet	화장, 몸단장, 변소 the act of dressing or grooming oneself, a bathroom
topple	앞으로 꼬꾸라지다 pitch; tumble down
traitor	속임수, 계략 a person who betrays another
tranquil	고요한 free from commotion or tumult; peaceful; quiet; calm
tranquillity	고요, 평안 calmness; peacefulness; quiet; serenity
transparent	투명한 clear; pellucid; limpid; crystalline
transport	황홀하게 하다 to carry away by strong emotion; enrapture
treachery	배신, 배신행위 an act of perfidy; faithlessness; treason
trickery	속임수, 계략 artifice; deception
tryst	연인끼리의 만남, 밀회 an appointment to meet somewhat secretly by lovers
tuck	쑤셔 넣다 to thrust in the loose end or edge of something
tuft	머리나 실 등의 다발 a bunch; cluster

tumult	떠들썩함, 폭동 uproar; general outbreak; riot; uprising
turmoil	동요, 혼란 confusion; disturbance
unbearable	견딜 수 없는 unendurable; intolerable
uncanny	으스스한, 기괴한, 불가사의한 arousing superstitious fear; mysterious
unique	독특한 unparalleled; incomparable
unperturbed	냉정한, 침착한 calm; serene; unruffled
untoward	온당치 못한 improper; unseemly
usurp	강탈하다, 불법 사용하다 to seize by force or without legal right
utmost	최고도의, 최대한 maximum, highest, foremost
vain	허영심이 강한, 공허한 egotistical; worthless
valiant	용맹한 brave; valorous; dauntless
vanish	사라지다 to disappear; go away
vehemently	격렬히 rancorously; angrily; violently
venom	악의, 원한, 독 malignity; acrimony; bitterness; poison
vermin	해충 noxious, objectionable, or disgusting animals
verse	시 a poem; piece of poetry
vexation	화남, 신경질 irritation; annoyance:

vibrate	진동하다 to quiver; tremble
vicious	악의가 있는 spiteful; malicious
victim	희생자 a person who is harmed or killed by another:
vigor	활력 healthy physical or mental energy or power; vitality
vile	비열한 depraved; despicable
vintage	수확기,~년식(처음 수확한 것) a year or period of origin
virulence	독성 the quality of being poisonous
voluntary	자발적인 of one's own accord or by free choice:
vulgar	저속한 indecent; obscene; lewd
wake	지나간 자국 the path or course of anything
warily	주의 깊게 watchfully
well	(우물처럼) 솟아나다 to rise; spring; gush
whiff	냄새 등의 한번 풍기기 a slight trace of odor or smell
withered	시들다(wither) to shrivel; fade; decay
wreath	화환 a garland; chaplet
yearn	그리워하다 to have an earnest or strong desire; long
yield	내주다 to give up or over; relinquish or resign

Summarize

Summarize

Summarize

Summarize

Summarize

Summarize

Summarize

Summarize